MW00775450

Anay's Will to Learn

BY ELAINE M. HAMPTON WITH
ANAY PALOMEQUE DE CARRILLO

Anay's Will to Learn

A WOMAN'S EDUCATION IN THE
SHADOW OF THE MAQUILADORAS

University of Texas Press AUSTIN

Requests for permission to reproduce material from this work
should be sent to:
    Permissions
    University of Texas Press
    P.O. Box 7819
    Austin, TX 78713–7819
    http://utpress.utexas.edu/about/book-permissions

⊗ The paper used in this book meets the minimum requirements of
ANSI/NISO Z39.48–1992 (R1997) (Permanence of Paper).

LIBRARY OF CONGRESS CATALOGING-IN-PUBLICATION DATA

Hampton, Elaine M., 1948–
    Anay's will to learn : a woman's education in the shadow of the
Maquiladoras / By Elaine M. Hampton with Anay Palomeque de
Carrillo.
        p   cm
    Includes bibliographical references and index.
    ISBN 978-0-292-74426-4 (cloth: alk. paper)
    1. Women—Education—Mexico.   2. Women—Mexico—Social
conditions.   3. Offshore assembly industry—Mexico.   I. Carrillo,
Anay Palomeque de.   II. Title.
    LC1772.H36   2013
    305.420972—dc23   2012032675

doi:10.7560/744264

Dedicated to Eva, Juliet, Elaincita, Kiké, Callye, John, Sophie, Addie, and Tate with the hope for a future full of cross-cultural communications for mutual learning and mutual benefit.

Contents

Acknowledgments

Many women helped in this effort. We express our appreciation to them for the many times they reviewed a section of the draft and shared their recommendations and comments to bring this book to light: Elsa Villa, Christine Eber, Mimi Wallace, Laura Self, Erika Mein, and Susan Brown.

Anay's Will to Learn

Introduction

*A*nay's *Will to Learn* explores education in an era of dramatic social and economic upheaval in rural and urban Mexico. The guide through that exploration is a young woman, Anay Palomeque de Carrillo,[1] who lived in Ciudad Juárez, Chihuahua, during the early years of the city's renowned violence. Ciudad Juárez[2] is a city in Mexico on the U.S. border in close proximity to El Paso, Texas. For most of their history, the two cities were one, separated by the river (once mighty, now a dry bed most of the year) and so close that, from my window on campus at the University of Texas at El Paso, I can see houses and cars on the sandy hills of Ciudad Juárez. I met Anay in the early 2000s during a period in my life when I was employed as a university professor and educational researcher in El Paso and conducting research in Ciudad Juárez and other Mexican cities. She became my guide into the lives of the Mexican factory workers, and we became friends. Over the years, she shared with me a myriad of experiences that revealed her determined pursuit of education while negotiating the complex social and cultural forces opposing her educational goals.

Two primary sources of information feed the book: Anay's story and my commentary on the sociopolitical context of the Mexican experience. The central piece of the book is Anay's story and is drawn from the original data—Anay's words, Anay's experiences, and my direct observations of her life in Mexico. Anay leads us through her experiences as a young girl in rural Southern Mexico, attending school under a mango tree and walking to neighboring communities to sell fruits and sweets from a basket on her head. In later chapters, we learn about her migration to Ciudad Juárez, her work in a maquiladora, her secondary education, and her triumph over physical and mental abuse, violence, and traumas inherent in low-income communities on the margins of social privilege. At the end of each chapter, I provide an "Interpretive Context" section to elaborate on the sociopolitical background or to highlight research that informs Anay's narrative.

This introductory chapter draws mostly from research about Ciudad Juárez and the maquiladora industry, information that is necessary to provide a solid understanding of the social, historical, economic, and political factors that fed into this unique Mexican border city during the turbulent era when Anay lived there. The chapter begins with a discussion of my research methodology and theory, followed by a description of Ciudad Juárez in the context of an era dominated by maquiladoras and extreme violence.

This introduction, therefore, is heavy with data and sources to describe and explain the setting. The reader may opt to begin reading in Chapter 2, where Anay's story unfolds, and later revisit this introductory information to better understand the environment that surrounded the women in Juárez.

RESEARCH DESIGN AND METHODOLOGY

This book is a critical ethnographic case study designed to examine and describe education in light of the social life and culture of a woman in Mexico in the context of rural and urban Mexican families meeting basic needs and seeking improvement while constrained by limited financial resources. Karen O'Reilly (2009) defines *critical ethnography* as "an approach that is overtly political and critical, exposing inequalities in an effort to effect change" (p. 51). Brown and Dobrin (2004) state that critical ethnography shifts the goal away from "the acquisition of knowledge about the Other . . . to the formation of a dialogic relationship with the Other whose destination is the social transformation of material conditions that immediately oppress, marginalize, or otherwise subjugate the ethnographic participant" (p. 5). In the present study, inequalities are exposed and social transformations emerge from the context and the dialogic relationship between Anay and me.

The original data that inform the case study come from my notes from the conversations, experiences, and events that Anay and I shared over these years. To situate these data, we provide information about the context of Anay's experiences, such as the maquiladora work experience, various forms of violence that she encountered, and certain aspects of Mexican education. I kept an ongoing journal recording all of the experiences we shared and Anay's verbal accounts of events in her life. I did not use a tape recorder for the interviews but tried to be as faithful to the individual's wording as possible. I am almost six feet tall, with blond hair, and my physical presence can be an intrusion in a Mexican community. Therefore, I opted to avoid the additional intrusion of a tape recorder.

The process of interviewing, listening, and learning from an individual over an extended period becomes intimate, and the participant and researcher's relationship becomes one of the multiple realities in the study. Anay's world was a stark contrast to my own, and in our interactions I encountered rare, adrenaline-soaked experiences that contributed to the narrative. My intervention was an influence on the story, and my voice is inherent in the story. The author's voice is more evident in feminist ethnography than in objective, positivist research. Geertz (1988), an acclaimed ethnographer, devotes an entire book to the value of the author's voice in the ethnographic study. That said, I do attempt to elevate Anay's narrative without losing the multiple realities evolving from our friendship and our experiences.[3]

Anay is in the early stages of learning English, and, though I tried to stay true to her stories, much of this account is told in my words. Therefore, the reality lies somewhere underneath Anay's memories, the stories she told to me, my language translations, my interpretation and perceptions, and my intervention in her life. The hard sciences can measure layers of ice to determine a precise year span or use specialized tools to quantify the exact amount of stress on a beam supporting a bridge. But true histories and accounts of biological interactions are much more organic, complex, and elusive. Examining the complexities of lives, experiences, and interactions among living organisms provides valuable information at a depth that leads to understanding. Yet there will remain what Ofelia Schutte (2000) calls "a residue of meaning that will not be reached in cross-cultural endeavors, a residue sufficiently important to point to what I shall refer to more abstractly as a principle incommensurability" (p. 49).

During the eight years of my study, I crossed often from El Paso, Texas, into Mexico to visit with Anay and her family in their home and in other community settings. In the first years, I was doing research on the schools and communities where these factory laborers lived in the border city of Ciudad Juárez, as well as in several other cities in the interior of Mexico. Anay and her husband, Enrique, became my guides, helping me navigate through the very big city of Ciudad Juárez to gain admission to the factories, schools, and workers' communities. We spent many days in these locations conducting interviews and observing in the schools.

As I learned more about Anay's life and her persistent pursuit of education, I joked that perhaps her life should be a new book. She loved the idea and began providing me with story after story that she wanted in her book. She is an eloquent woman who tells engaging stories. After every visit, I rushed to the computer to document the story as true to her telling as possible and to record my notes and reflections. Anay and her family came to El Paso often to shop or meet their church friends, so we used these opportunities to visit. Sometimes, when they could, they would spend the weekend with me, and Anay and I would stay up to talk after our families had gone to bed. I bought her a computer so we could e-mail back and forth. In the summer of 2008 I had a little research money, so Anay and I traveled to her childhood home in the south of Mexico. There we visited her family, friends, and teachers, and I learned much about the context of her young life in this rural area.

After several years and volumes and volumes of notes, a thematic structure began to emerge. I discussed this with Anay. I gave her copies of the drafts. They were written in English, so I provided rough oral translations. She pored over the drafts with her dictionary and called or e-mailed me from time to time to offer a correction or suggestion, twice requesting that I eliminate a segment that she thought did not portray her accurately. I eliminated those segments. And thus, two authors shaped the story.

THEORETICAL FOUNDATION: POSTCOLONIAL FEMINIST THEORY

This work contributes to other studies in cross-cultural communication founded in postcolonial feminist theory. Repeatedly, and often blatantly, evident in this study are the oppressive powers exerted over women, in particular Mexican women, living within the poverty traps of border factory environments. The legacy of Spanish colonial practices, along with sudden and powerful social upheavals riding the wave of neo-liberal[4] market practices dictated by international trade agreements, has spawned oppression, marginalization, and violence for many Latin Americans, but for women especially. The oppression is characterized by not simply lack of choices but such a limitation of options that individuals are often denied the ability to effectively promote their own good (Schutte, 2000).

Anay is a woman who met that oppression with uncompromising resolve and achieved her education in ways unheard-of for those of us north of the Mexican border. She becomes our guide through cultural differences; she is, as Ofelia Schutte (2000) describes, ". . . that person or experience which makes it possible for the self to recognize its own limited horizons in the light of asymmetrically given relations marked by sexual, social, cultural, or other differences" (p. 46).

It is the cross-cultural communication in this postcolonial feminist approach that allows us to examine the differences and "to reach new ethical, aesthetic, and political ground. . . . Post-colonial feminist theory, in its various manifestations, pays special attention to issues of language, class, and racial, ethnic, sexual, and gender differences, to the justification of narratives about the nation-state" (Schutte, 2000, p. 46).

When we examine them from the level of the populations outside the circles of power and privilege, we see that neoliberal market practices have the power to revive the social abuses of colonization. Poverty in Mexico became more acute during the late 1980s when then President Carlos Salinas de Gotari opened the country to liberal economic policies such as those outlined in the North American Free Trade Agreement (NAFTA). These practices shifted many government-sponsored programs out of the public realm and into private enterprises where they would be restructured as businesses seeking profit. Before that time, there were many small community-owned farms that provided minimal but sustainable income. New legislation to accommodate NAFTA allowed the private sale of the community parcels, thus reducing these individuals' ability to provide food and income to meet their daily needs. This unleashed a flood of impoverished Mexicans moving to the northern border to work in the factories and to try to cross the border to work in the United States. These migrations led them to the margins of their geographic world as well as the margins of their social worlds; thus, they became more vulnerable to abuse and violence (Floyd, 2010).[5]

The maquiladora program, discussed in more depth later,

is also a direct result of the economic restructuring defined by NAFTA. I do not deny that many people have benefited from NAFTA, and any researcher can find documentation of positive progress for some Mexican and U.S. citizens. Nevertheless, there is ample evidence that the lives of millions of Mexicans, mostly those in rural and/or impoverished settings, have been subject to economic and social changes resulting from NAFTA that were detrimental to their livelihood.

Mexicans who lost their farms and jobs moved north, hoping to find work. Moving with them were their traditional understandings about men's and women's roles, with women carrying out domestic duties and men in labor outside of the home. In many cases, women now found themselves in wage-earning positions, and families were left to deal with the sudden upheaval of an ancient social structure. This led to further oppression of women as the factory labor culture exposed them to abusive working conditions and very low wages. Anay's story is evidence, and the deadly violence against women in Ciudad Juárez is a result.

Anay's experience working in the maquiladoras and her close calls with violence in the city will be explained in later chapters. But first we need an overview of the historical and political influences that have led Ciudad Juárez to its status in 2011 as the most violent city in the world (Cardona, 2012).

A CITY IN A SOCIAL EARTHQUAKE

Ciudad Juárez perches on an allegorical fault line as one of the world's richest nations scrapes against a young, still developing nation. The northern borderlands of Mexico have long suffered and will continue to suffer from social, environmental, and economical tremors and quakes because of their proximity to the United States. The maquiladora industry initiated the tremors with its super-exploitation through low pay and poor working conditions and its instant restructuring of centuries-old customs in traditional Mexican home life and family roles. Immigration from the interior was fueled by the maquiladoras' bringing packed vanloads and busloads of Mexicans from the southern states. Population in the border regions exploded.

Stressed infrastructure resources cause more tremors and quakes. Water sources are very limited and rapidly being depleted in the high desert, which sits at about 4,000 feet elevation and receives about eight inches of rainfall per year. In addition, the city strains under the stress of extremely rapid growth without sufficient resources for paved roads, utilities, wastewater treatment, garbage removal, health care, schools, and adequate housing. These social upheavals—the U.S. recession and the unemployment it caused in Ciudad Juárez, the poverty, and the tedium and abuses experienced by people working in factory jobs—have contributed greatly to the social instability of the city.

Historical Causes of the Instability

The history of Ciudad Juárez provides insight into some of the reasons why, today, it sits on such shaky ground. Mexico is a young nation. Its recent history is mostly one of outside domination. Colonization wreaked havoc on indigenous Mexico. Jack Weatherford (1988) documents in detail the abuses of the Spanish conquest of Latin America, providing many examples of how the wealth of human and natural resources were stripped away in the conquerors' quest for riches, fame, and religious domination. When Mexico finally became independent from Spain in 1821, it still suffered years of unrest as self-government was in the early stages of development. Then a devastating and humiliating war with the United States resulted in the loss of close to half of Mexico's land—much of the southwestern United States, including Texas and California. In the 1860s France invaded and set up a short-lived empire, and later political instability led to a costly revolution. A democratic system of government was set up in 1917, but interpreting and implementing that system has proved challenging. A democratic Mexico is fewer than one hundred years old and still defining itself.

Among the several interesting books that chronicle the history of Ciudad Juárez is *Crónica en el desierto* (Flores Simental, Gutiérrez Roa, and Vázquez Reyes, 1998). The authors explain some historical events that shaped the city, a city far removed from its state and national capitals and much closer to U.S. influences. Before 1900, Ciudad Juárez and El Paso functioned informally as one city, with citizens passing over the river bridges freely. Then, in the early decades of 1900, a Mexican civil war forced many businesses on the Mexican side to move into El Paso. The cities began to divide, and the chasm between their resources deepened as the businesses in Ciudad Juárez were left with fewer and fewer options.

The authors mention that Ciudad Juárez is a desert city built on thirst. It was an early center for mining activities in the surrounding mountains in Mexico and the United States, so miners used it as a retreat. It had one of the early soft drink bottling businesses, and I remember crossing into the city when I was a little girl to buy a case of Coke, much less expensive than we could get at home and, in our opinion, much sweeter. During prohibition in the United States, Ciudad Juárez responded to the demand for a product that was prohibited in the United States, and the entertainment sector grew as it catered to U.S. citizens who wanted a night out with alcoholic drinks. As the military bases and universities developed in El Paso and New Mexico, soldiers and college students took advantage of the many bars and the night life. Ciudad Juárez also had a horse racing track and a bull ring providing entertainment that was not available in the nearby United States.

These valuable income streams were quickly followed by detrimental, often illegal, activities and businesses, and they still exist today. Bars, saloons, and gambling nurtured activities based on greed and corruption such as prostitution, human trafficking, and drugs. These were fueled by the lack of employment for the city's residents as well as the many restless Mexicans from elsewhere who waited in the city for a chance to cross to the United States. People from the interior come to the border, gambling on a wispy hope: *Maybe I'll win the lottery, or maybe I'll be able to cross into the land of plenty. Or maybe I'll meet a man from the United States in one of the bars; maybe we'll fall in love and get married. Or maybe I'll get a good job in Ciudad Juárez and stay.*

Charles Bowden (2010), a highly recognized chronicler of border events, reports in his book *Murder City*:

> Juárez has long supplied Americans with what they wanted—booze during Prohibition, women at all times, opiates when they were outlawed in the United States, quick divorces when the marriages soured—and like the rest of Mexico, the city has operated as a partnership between criminal organizations and government. Geography has made the city the link between the center of Mexico and the transportation arteries of the United States. But in the 1980s, major cocaine routes shifted from Florida to Mexico, and Juárez became the beneficiary of this change . . . this city . . . it is built not of bricks and mortar but of narco-dollars. (pp. 207–208)

In the twentieth century, El Paso and Ciudad Juárez functioned as sister cities—very unequal sisters, but still communicating freely. Thousands of El Paso residents had family in Ciudad Juárez and crossed often to visit. Children lived for months or years in one city and then crossed to live in the other city, and then back again. Besides the maquiladoras, there were many businesses with extensions on both sides of the border. People living in Ciudad Juárez would cross into El Paso to shop or have a nice dinner, and El Pasoans would cross into Ciudad Juárez for the same reasons.

As of 2011, cross-border experiences are almost nonexistent. I do informal surveys with my students at the University of Texas at El Paso. Previously, when asked how many reg-

ularly visited family and friends in Ciudad Juárez, more than
50 percent of the hands went up. Now, very few cross the border.
They are left to mourn for their family members who remain
in Ciudad Juárez, trapped in their houses, afraid to be seen on
the streets. Or those in Juárez cross to live with family in El
Paso and nearby communities. Those who have crossed but do
not have legal papers also feel trapped in their homes, afraid to
step outside because Border Patrol agents may be roaming the
neighborhoods.

Political Causes of the Instability

In 2008 and 2009, the violence in Ciudad Juárez and other
border cities escalated to a crisis level as drug gangs battled for
dominance. President George W. Bush's administration tight-
ened border control between Mexico and the United States
through stricter security at the border check stations and the
creation of 700 miles of a series of fifteen-feet-high metal walls
along the border. As the drug industry butted up against tighter
barriers, the drug trade concentrated in Mexico's northern border cities. In addition, President Felipe Calderón declared a war
on drugs during his first weeks in office and sent large numbers
of soldiers to border cities. I remember crossing the bridge in
downtown Ciudad Juárez and passing by hundreds of soldiers
lining the street—very young men in full protective gear standing in the 100-degree heat. In Ciudad Juárez the military intrusion stirred up drug-related resistance, and the violence continued to escalate.

Jorge Castañeda (2010) a well-known authority on Mexican politics, supports the claim that the president's war escalated the violence on the border. He also shares other insights
into the causes for the failure of the Mexican war on drugs and
states that the causes and solutions are closely tied to the U.S.
failed war on drugs—drugs that are demanded almost exclu-
sively from U.S. consumers to feed an almost bottomless hun-
ger. Tim Padgett (2011) of *Time* magazine supports Castañeda's

position that U.S. actions have supported the growth of the drug trade in Mexico and describes the cycles of increased drug trafficking following on the heels of ill-conceived U.S. political action in Mexico. It began in 1969, when President Richard Nixon declared a war on drugs and demanded action from Mexico, resulting in massive policing along the border. That action was interpreted in Mexico as international extortion, and, instead of curbing the flow of drugs, it caused violence, anger, and new motivation for the drug suppliers.

Most U.S. presidential administrations since that time have implemented some kind of Mexican antidrug policy —"tough on drugs" gets votes. Over the years, the implementation of these U.S. interventions, often knee-jerk political actions, affected Mexican society in numerous ways, although the U.S. leaders had little information about the problems they were aiming to attack. The latest such intervention was the Mérida Initiative. In 2008, the United States committed $1.3 billion to Mexico for counter-drug and anti-crime assistance. The Congressional Research Service Report on the Mérida Initiative (Seelke, 2010) relates concern about the success of this program, with its lack of a focus on reducing demand for the drugs. In Ciudad Juárez I found no evidence of success of the Mérida Initiative.

These political actions increased pressure on the drug trade, thereby escalating the price of the drugs. Many have benefited from that increased price tag—the cartels, the funeral directors, the U.S. bankers who launder the money, the businesses who front the money laundering, the U.S. security consultants and border guards, the military contractors on both sides of the border, and politicians who sell sound bites about the vastly complex problem and win votes because of their convincing but shallow spin on the truth.

By about 2009, the economic recession generated by the banking industry in the United States joined the drug war to swing a double blow to Ciudad Juárez. Maquiladoras dropped production levels or closed entirely. *Frontera NorteSur* (2009) reported that about 80,000 of the 250,000 factory jobs were lost in

2009. These numbers actually were much worse, as most facto-ries put their employees on reduced work weeks, often only half time, a phenomenon not counted in the official numbers of jobs lost. The violence continued escalating through 2010. Weekly body counts in the tens and twenties appeared in the local me-dia, with a total of more than 3,000 murders for the year (Car-dona, 2012). Those who could afford to do so abandoned their homes and moved to the interior of Mexico, and many U.S. cit-izens who lived in that city relocated to El Paso or other loca-tions nearby. El Milenio.com, a Mexican news outlet (Becera-Acosta, 2010), reported that, as of early 2010, more than 500,000 citizens, almost 40 percent of the population, had left the city and 25 percent of homes were abandoned. Most of those aban-doned homes were vandalized. Scores of citizens were in grave danger and seeking asylum in El Paso.

Luis Herrera Robles (2007) posits that national, state, and local government agencies stepped aside and allowed the ma-quiladora industry to fill the important roles that government should have provided in the city, a phenomenon he calls *des-gobierno*, or disgovernment. The Mexican and U.S. policy mak-ers sat back and observed or, worse, ignored the upheaval of social order in the wake of the maquiladora industry and the lack of basic infrastructure support that these huge changes de-manded. Schools, water, roads, transportation, housing, and medical services dangled slowly and weakly after the maquila-dora boom and the waves of immigrants it brought. With the economic downturns, the "disgovernment" left a vacuum that was readily filled with gang rivalries and drug trafficking.[6]

Thus, the governmental abandonment, the lack of infra-structure, the rapid population shifts, the social upheavals, the U.S. recession, extreme unemployment, the gender imbalance, the poverty, the tedium of the factory jobs, the city's role in sup-plying drugs to the U.S. market along with its history of serv-ing U.S. citizens in their demands for risky entertainment—all together they shook the society so hard that a quake of murder and torture resulted. Mexico's northern neighbors are far from innocent in creating that quake, and the tremors will surely spill into those societies.

This brings to mind Mary Shelley's *Frankenstein*, which is more than a good horror story; it is a feminist exploration of the concern that Western scientific and technological inventions create monsters that attack segments of society. As Anay's story reveals, the maquiladora movement that brought her to Ciudad Juárez is a creation of U.S. economic and technological advancement. The violence that it spawned is a result of the giant metallic feel of the wheels of these industries grinding through a fragile and vulnerable social structure, tumbling a society that was dependent on its rich neighbor, even as that neighbor withdrew the structure it helped to build.

HISTORY AND CONTEXT OF
THE MAQUILADORA INDUSTRY

In the late 1960s, foreign factories started locating in Mexico to take advantage of the low labor wages and tax breaks. Japan, Germany, Korea, Mexico, and other countries set up maquiladoras in Mexico, but the majority of the factories were U.S. firms, mostly Fortune 500 businesses. While driving in the city, I remember seeing plants for General Electric, General Motors, Whirlpool, Honeywell, Lear Corporation, Electrolux, Johnson & Johnson, 3M, Siemens, Federal Mogul, Epson, and Bosch. Usually raw materials or partially completed parts are shipped to Mexico to be assembled into a partially or fully completed product and then shipped back to the country of origin. This back-and-forth has allowed corporations to circumvent taxes (González Boz, 1993). About 65 percent of this assembly line industry is located near the U.S. border; the rest is in other regions of Mexico. By 2010, Ciudad Juárez had the largest number of maquiladora employees in the nation, up to 250,000 jobs in more than 300 factories.

The U.S.-Mexico labor relationship in the context of maquiladora industry was not the first situation in which U.S. economic interests saw a large financial benefit in using Mexicans as a source of labor. In the early 1900s, an agreement between the two countries allowed Mexicans to work in U.S. agriculture under certain conditions. This *bracero* program ended in the 1960s and caused increased unemployment in the border regions as these laborers and some of their families had relocated in northern Mexico and were stranded there when the program ended.

Mexico allowed the maquiladora industry to locate in border towns with the hope that it would ease unemployment. However, companies had only one reason for locating a factory in Mexico: to increase corporate profits, mostly through reduced labor costs. A factory may employ one thousand to two thousand people, 80 percent of whom are line workers. In the United States, each line worker's salary would be more than $10.00 per hour. In Mexico, the same work is accomplished for about $4.50 to $6.00 per day (Kopinak, 1996). Bowden (2010) states that wages with benefits were closer to $10.00 to $12.00 per day. The individuals whom I interviewed quoted take-home daily pay averaging closer to $6.00 for the years 2003–2007.[7]

The maquiladora industry waxes and wanes in rhythm with the U.S. economy. In 2003, in response to the weakened U.S. economy, many of the factories in Ciudad Juárez closed and 60,000 to 80,000 workers were out of work. When the economy strengthened in 2005, hiring resurged. Then, in 2008, the U.S. recession caused even greater factory closures and unemployment. A common statement on the border is that when the United States sneezes, Mexico gets the flu.

The industry does provide benefits that attract workers. Maquiladora employees are eligible to participate in the nation's socialized medicine program. The factory pays about half of the enrollment fee and the employees pay about half, depending on their wages. Some people work in the maquiladoras just so that they can have these medical benefits for their families, as other family income may come from private employment. However, this also means that there are throngs of people waiting to enter the city's clinics.

In addition to medical benefits, the factories have provided some valuable contributions to employees. Some Mexicans, like Anay, come to the U.S.-Mexico border and the maquiladoras because the opportunities for them or their children to attend school are greater there, although still very limited, than in the rural areas to the south. The Davol factory mentioned in chapter 5 is the only factory I encountered that provided education beyond basic job training for some of its line workers. During the early years of the industry, before the peso devaluation, the pay was often higher, about the equivalent of U.S. sixty dollars per week (Kopinak, 1996). For some women, this provided an opportunity preferable to the traditional options of working the fields, serving as a maid for another family, or enduring an abusive husband. Factory work allowed these women some degree of independence with health care, occasional benefits, and a little higher social status than they would have if they were serving as maids.

In my earlier research on Mexican education in these factory communities (Hampton, 2004), I found a real economic benefit for individuals hired by the maquiladoras to fill jobs in mid-level technical, engineering, and management positions. These employees, mostly men, received professional development, educational benefits, and a salary that put them near the middle-class level of Mexican society. Perhaps the most valuable direct result of the maquiladora industry is this increase in the quality and quantity of better-paid technical and administrative jobs, which are held by 15 to 20 percent of the 1.5 million factory employees across Mexico (Kopinak, 1996).

I visited several U.S. maquiladoras and did not witness any "sweatshop" kind of treatment. In these automobile parts and clothing factories, employees were treated similarly to those in the United States. U.S. manufacturers are held publicly accountable by authorities in both countries for appropriate lighting, temperature, work hours, etc. The factories must meet strict guidelines for vacation (usually six days a year), hiring ages, overtime, and breaks. There is some transparency in the operations as many employees are U.S. citizens living in El Paso. I have taught several students who are current or past maquiladora employees. Friends work in the maquiladoras—in leadership as well as in the assembly lines. Knowing my interest in this field, we have open conversations about the industry. There is no reference to sweatshop labor or hazardous work conditions. I am confident in saying that most working conditions in U.S. plants that I visited in Ciudad Juárez do meet the set standards. Other authors have documented much harsher treatment, and some of those sources are referenced below.

ABUSES IN THE INDUSTRY

That said, meeting the required working conditions does not equal a good work environment or employee benefit, and many abuses still occur. The most dangerous of these is ridiculously low wages. Martínez and McCaughan (1990) use the term *super-exploitation* to refer to a practice that "violates the value of labor power[,] . . . payment of labor below its value" (p. 36). As discussed earlier, factory labor wages are very low—the equivalent of about four to nine U.S. dollars per day. The line workers take home a fraction of what a family needs to meet basic needs at a cost of living just slightly lower than that in the United States (Arriola, 2001).

Child care is seldom provided in the factories, so workers must depend on friends or extended family to watch their children during their shifts. Paying for child care is out of the question. Some of the new immigrants do not have family or friends to help care for their children. The principal of a school serving factory workers in Ciudad Juárez told me that many mothers had to make the difficult decision to either work in the factory to feed their children or stay home to take care of their children; they could not do both. Luis Reygadas's 1992 work on maquiladora workers in Chihuahua provides information similar to what this principal reported.

Arriola (2001) provides a view into the lives of maquiladora workers in the chemical plants near Acuña, a Mexican city across from Del Rio, Texas:

> There is the emotional and visual impact of visiting a maquiladora worker in a home that may or may not have a toilet, that has walls and ceilings made of cardboard, wood and metal castoffs, as she tells you about co-workers nearly losing fingers and hands to job accidents, spontaneous abortions and poor medical care, or just how she and her family are trying to eke out an existence on the insulting wages that typify the global economy's 'race to the bottom.' (p. 3)

The second great injustice is the industry's massive relocation of potential workers and their families to areas that lack the infrastructure these people need. The attraction of this employment caused Ciudad Juárez to balloon from about 280,000 people in 1960 to more than 1.3 million in 2005 (Peña and Fuentes, 2007). Other border cities' populations exploded as well. My colleagues at one of the universities in Ciudad Juárez told me that, during the rapid growth of the 1990s, sometimes six buses full of workers were arriving each day from the state of Veracruz alone. The bus drivers dropped the new employees at the doors of the maquiladora for their first day on the job, and, often, these new migrants were left to find housing on their own. From Anay's and her mother's experiences, we know that vans and buses also regularly brought people from other states in the interior of Mexico. The laborers settled in makeshift housing in the desert and on the mountainsides on the outskirts of the city, paying part of their meager fees to opportunists who sold parcels of land at high prices. These emerging communities have minimal, if any, infrastructure. The homes are built of temporary materials such as tires, packing pallets, and old automobile parts. The residents of these peripheral communities are far from services and must depend on inefficient bus systems for long trips to purchase necessities.

A colleague of mine works in an organization that provides infrastructure to the businesses building new factories in Mexico. He told me this story but requested that I keep confidential his identity and that of the company involved. A large manufacturer was selecting from two locations near the border for its very large auto assembly factory. One location was in a very small town several miles from a population center, which would require that many workers move to this new area. My friend was hired to provide an assessment of what it would cost if the factory provided roads, water, electricity, and schools to the new community that would emerge. He made the assessment and provided the financial spreadsheet to the factory administrators. The cost was more than they wanted to pay. Nevertheless, the large company built the factory in that small town, provided nothing for infrastructure, and left the workers to manage on their own.

Another form of abuse in the factories occurs through employee-to-employee harassment. The foreign owners depend on Mexican managers and may not get involved in their management style, leaving openings for sexual harassment and threats from low-level managers to their line workers. María Fernández-Kelly (1983) provides examples of such harassment from guards and others, such as those individuals in charge of hiring employees. One of her contacts provided the account of a man who hired women employees and passed himself as a doctor so he could sexually abuse the women during their "check-ups." There are anecdotal reports of managers and security guards in the maquiladoras involved in the selection of young women who have been abducted, tortured, and murdered. Moreover, the piecework nature of factories generates tension between the line workers. Workers receive bonuses for meeting quotas, and if the woman who works the piece before you is slow, your production slows and your tension grows.

Prieto's research in Tijuana factories in the 1990s provides insight into how women were trapped in social power plays that occurred in factories that were run by well-intended managers who had no understanding of what can happen in a setting where women are desperate for their daily pay and any tiny hope for advancement. One participant, Marta, gave this account:

> The supervisor takes to flirting with me saying, "You're the best worker, and that's why you're my favorite." Soon all the women are jealous because he treats me better than them, and they all stop talking to me. After several days he says the same thing to another, and all the women get jealous again. We are always competing to be the best and become the favorite. Every day the girls go to work more and more decked out, and no sooner do we complain about something we don't like than the bosses tell us, "Arguing is not ladylike; if you get angry it makes you unattractive, and then we won't be fond of you." (Iglesias Prieto, 1997, p. 76)

Another detriment to employees is that factory assembly work is difficult and often tedious and uncomfortable. These low-end jobs, because of their routine, dead-end nature, are not advantageous to women (Stromquist and Monkman, 2000). Of course, this is not unique to Mexican factories; each kind of work in different regions across the globe brings its own set of discomforts. Anay's mother told how her feet hurt from standing long hours on the factory floor, and some of the women who worked for the vacuum cleaner plant said they did not like the tedium of screwing the same components together over and over for eight hours a day. I visited a factory in the Mexican state of Puebla where athletic garments for U.S. sports stores were cut and assembled. I witnessed the employees, mostly women, working in a comfortable, well-lit factory. They received adequate lunch and rest breaks. However, every woman had a large stack of the same section of a garment on her machine. For her eight-hour shift, she sewed the same seams repeatedly and passed the piece to her neighbor to sew her set of seams, and thus the piece went down the line, growing into a complete garment. María Fernández-Kelly (1983) worked in a factory for several months as part of her study. She was expected to sew pockets on jeans—360 per hour, or about 3,000 per shift. Norma Iglesias Prieto (1997) documents women's accounts of health issues that resulted from repetitive movement or from their contact with metals and chemicals. The women requested medical services for these health issues but were ignored. They said that this made them feel that they were used up and were easily replaced.

Additional benefits are used in growth times as incentives to woo new employees or to prevent "job hopping." The factories may provide tutoring services, transportation, lunches, sports and recreational programs, clinics and birth control pills, child care, and even allowances for housing and groceries. These benefits are not common, they may disappear altogether when the supply of employees is greater than the demand, and they can be used as rewards or punishments for attendance or tardiness. Anay's account of her educational experience at the maquiladora is an example of how these benefits can be used in abusive ways.

An additional advantage afforded to corporations is that fewer and looser union regulations in Mexico often speed production output. Thus production efficiency may come at the employees' expense in shortcuts that affect health and safety. Mexican law requires that employees who give birth be given twelve weeks' paid leave and guaranteed their job when they return, with two half-hour breaks for breast-feeding (Kopinak, 1996). I have heard anecdotal reports of women having to prove they are menstruating to keep their jobs so the factory will not have to provide maternity leave. There is little union support in the maquiladoras in Ciudad Juárez, so job security is tenuous. Moreover, some managers accept bribes to bypass implementing standards in human resources or environmental safety. It is also likely that some small factories stay hidden and avoid regulations by not registering with the authorities.

During the Spanish colonization of Mexico, Spanish women

were "sheltered, patronized and protected" (Hart, 1980, p. 151) from the world full of indigenous people bending under their conquerors. The indigenous women, on the other hand, were treated as harshly as their men in working conditions. Mexico became industrialized during the second half of the nineteenth century, and men and women from lower-income backgrounds entered the factories. Women were paid less. Employees organized and the union structures continually fought, and sometimes won, fairer labor practices. Few factory laborers in the border cities are unionized. A website designed to attract new manufacturers to the city announces that only 5 percent of the employees in Ciudad Juárez are members of a union (TeamNAFTA.com). Tiano (1994) and Peña (1997) document the strength of women in the factories as they build informal networks of resistance to the power structures inherent in this unequal labor relationship. Del Castillo (1980) credits this kind of exploitation to the antagonistic relationship between the working class and the capitalist.

> The personal, sociopolitical, and economic oppression of women contributes directly and indirectly to the power of capitalist oppression . . . their exploitation has direct consequences for all workers when female labor is used to hold down wages, prevent unionization, maintain insufferable working conditions, or replace the labor of strikers . . . Interpersonal oppression of women, whether intentional or not, in effect, only reinforces this devaluation." (p. 13)

In the early years of the maquiladora industry, it was mostly women who were hired to work the assembly lines, for such insulting reasons as that they were more compliant, that they would not unionize, that they were more agile, and that they were more attractive. Advertisements for employment often mentioned that the company was hiring single, young, attractive women. During that period, hundreds of buses and vans brought thousands of young women to the border, so that today there are many more women in the city than men. In those earlier years, and to some extent today, this created a fishbowl setting—pretty young women working under the close observation and power of men, depending on these men for approval to keep their jobs. Today, there is more balance on the line; however, more men than women fill the middle and higher management positions (Salzinger, 2003).

I scan the Ciudad Juárez daily newspaper, *El Diario*, from time to time. Of course, in 2010 there are very few jobs listed in the employment section. On occasion I see a job posting that is requesting either a male or female, and sometimes the posting will provide an age range. But the large U.S. maquiladoras currently do not post advertisements for single, young, attractive women.

In my visits inside the factories, I met with maquiladora managers who were aware of the gender inequity in higher management and technician positions. Two of them stated that they work to create more gender balance. They encounter difficulties in finding enough women with the qualifications who would apply for those jobs. This gender issue is more broadly encompassing as Mexican education and social conditions are not in step with the rapidly growing, technologically saturated employment needs around the globe.[8]

The world of maquiladora employment is vast, with practices that vary greatly in the treatment of employees, and these practices change (we have seen some improvement) over time. It is not fair to condemn the practice all together, and some studies in the field of economics, along with my previous research, show a contribution to Mexican society through improved employment and education for a subset of the employees. However, the consistent and well-documented abuses remain: extremely low pay for the line workers evident in almost every factory and the seismic-like tremors that result when populations are shifted from southern Mexico to the border, where roles within families are turned upside down. This creates a shaky substratum in the city—a large section of society living in extreme poverty.

People are subject to more hardships and abuses because of that poverty and because they are foreign to the city. For most of its inhabitants, Ciudad Juárez does not wear the title of home and thus misses out on that sense of place, purpose, commitment, and community spirit that homes enjoy.

ONE

Meeting Anay

In the border areas, churches often serve as vehicles for cross-border connections and collaborations. My home, Las Cruces, New Mexico, is about forty miles up the Rio Grande from Ciudad Juárez. In 2002 a friend who is a member of the Church of Christ in Las Cruces invited me to go with a group from her church to visit another Church of Christ in Ciudad Juárez. The purpose of the trip was to worship with the Mexican church on Sunday morning and to visit with the church leaders about helping them replace a section of their roof. I had begun my research on the educational environment in Mexican maquiladora labor communities and was interested in the opportunity to meet some of the factory workers who lived near the church or attended it.

The church was located in the southern part of the city, just one block east of one of the major north-south arteries, a four-lane street lined with small businesses. We made sharp turns into the very narrow, unpaved, alley-like street, lined on our right with the high-security walls of the church, eight to nine feet tall, and on our left, the high-security walls of three private houses. At the south end of the street was a large *yonke*, an unofficial Spanish term for auto junkyard. In the past, used autos, languishing in the last months of their working life, slid from the U.S. side of the border into Ciudad Juárez; now they fill the *yonkes* that dot the roads near the outskirts of the city where land is less expensive. Current laws restrict the importation of older cars into Mexico. This *yonke* was a large fenced lot with metallic racks where the bodies of spent automobiles were stacked four high, visible and accessible to the customer looking for spare auto parts. The tires from these spent autos were piled into a dangerous black mountain that polluted the desert sands south of the city.

The solid metal gates in the church security wall were open, and we entered the small patio area where members conversed on their way into the church building. There, I saw Anay for the first time. The wife of a part-time minister, she was a busy young woman, interacting with the visitors and her fellow church members while holding a baby on her hip. Her face showed more Spanish features than Indian. Instead of the deep, rich black hair of many mestizos (people of mixed Indian and European ancestry), her hair was more of a chestnut brown. Instead of the deep coffee-brown eyes, her eyes had a little dance of hazel in them.

On this side of the privilege line, we women often open our conversations with a comment on a pair of shoes or a piece of jewelry. On a previous trip to a Mexican community, I had complimented a young woman on her earrings. She took the earrings from her ears, handed them to me, and insisted that I keep them. I later learned that this is a Mexican's very polite response to someone's compliment, so I stopped complimenting women on their jewelry. But I felt very comfortable connecting through cuddly babies, and before long, Anay's baby, Eva, and her soggy diaper were on my lap as the church service began. Soon the baby got restless, so I walked out the back door with her. Her mother followed me. We walked up and down the sandy road with baby Eva and visited while the church service continued inside. Anay told me that she and Enrique lived in one of the classrooms in the small church complex. Enrique was a part-time youth minister in the church, and he wanted to start a new church group in a low-income neighborhood in the sandy hills on the southern edge of the city.

We had not walked far when Anay said, "I am really smart

in school. Mostly, I love mathematics. I really want to finish my school and go to the university. I'm studying now on these books. When church is over, I'll take you into my room and show you my books. I have to read a lot of books and take a lot of tests, but I'm going to do it."

The soggy diaper was now overflowing. When church let out, we went into her little room for a quick diaper change. It really was a small Sunday school classroom filled up with a bed and some boxes lining the walls. The kind-hearted church leaders had allowed them to live here temporarily. A plastic dishpan and a few dishes were on a small table. She handed me three of her books. We sat on the bed to look at them. Each book covered one curriculum area for one semester of junior high school. She showed me Math III and English II. "I read every book and do the homework pages. See, here is my homework from yesterday. I answer all the questions. Then, I have to go to a little office—it's not too far—and I pay 30 pesos [about US$2.50]. There are thirty-four books for my junior high degree. I just have fourteen more to do."

That first encounter was in the summer. A few weeks later, our summer rainy season began, with its pattern of isolated thunderstorms. In this high desert, we get an average of eight inches of rain a year; however, most of that comes in July and August in two or three big storms. One of these three-inch rainstorms fell in the area of their church. The weight of the water collapsed part of the roof, right over Anay and Enrique's little room. Everything was soaked. In my visit a few weeks later, all their belongings were out in the patio area drying. She maintained a light attitude and joked as she showed me the damage. She held up their only wedding photo, badly stained by the water, and gave me a one-sided smile as she ran a finger over the damaged photo.

"Did I tell you that we rode the bus to our wedding? And that I was wearing this dress on the bus? [She laughed.] Enrique did have a little car, but someone ran into him and wrecked the car just two days before the wedding! That hurt his neck, so he was wearing a big neck brace and I was wearing my wedding dress and we rode the bus to the church. Everyone on the bus was smiling and clapping for us."

During this time when our friendship was young, Enrique was trying to feed and house his new family. The church in Ciudad Juárez provided their housing. He worked as their youth minister in return. He also worked in a maquiladora, and Anay was studying for her junior-high school degree through a take-home course and caring for the baby as well as helping around the church.

Anay and Enrique introduced me to some of their church friends who worked in the maquiladoras. At that time, the educational environment in these factories and the surrounding communities was the main focus of my research. As discussed in the introduction, the maquiladora industries have the power to concentrate poverty and to cause sudden shifts in population, sprouting hundreds of new settlements lacking important community infrastructure. In my research, I was examining how these corporate power surges were reflected in educational opportunities for the workers.

As an outsider, I felt that I could not navigate this foreign dimension alone. So I asked Anay and Enrique if I could hire them to be my guides. Through the next few years, we had many wild and exciting adventures driving around the periphery of the city on rutted roads full of sand traps. Nice people helped us get my car out of sand traps more than once (I learned to always carry an extra twenty-dollar bill), and we endured the desert heat, blinding spring sandstorms, and several flat tires. First baby Eva, then Eva and baby Juliet joined us in these adventures.

Then my research took an unexpected turn. As we were able to spend many hours together, Anay, knowing my interest in educational experiences in Mexico, began sharing more and more of her life stories with me. After each visit, I had time to mull over our conversations and experiences as I waited in line at the international border to cross back into the United States and as I drove to my office in El Paso, Texas, just across the border, or a few miles upriver to my home in Las Cruces. I would rush to the computer to document the words, events, and my thoughts. My research project became largely Anay's story.

Anay shared much information about her daily experiences in Ciudad Juárez and, from time to time, mentioned experiences and memories from her childhood home in southern Mexico. She described her grandparents' *ranchito* and the thatched-roof buildings where she grew up. Anay and Enrique, like many maquiladora workers in Ciudad Juárez, had moved to the border from a more southerly location in Mexico. My interactions with workers in the border region often left me asking myself, "What were their homes like before they moved to Ciudad Juárez? Why did they come here?" A funding opportunity came along for me to travel to conduct research, and I asked Anay if she would like to return to southern Mexico to show me her home. She was delighted. In July of 2008, we flew to southern Mexico, toured her childhood home, and visited many of her family members. Chapter 2 begins Anay's story with that visit to her rural home in tropical southern Mexico—a palm-topped structure an arm's length from nature. The chapter includes Anay's descriptions of her early life there along with her account of her responsibility, as a very young child, to provide income to the family by selling food products in neighboring communities. To help interpret her experience, I examine the phenomenon of child labor in informal markets.

Chapter 3 provides information on schooling in southern Mexico, mostly through the interview with Anay's teachers. We do not attempt to describe the complex system that is Mexican schooling but do provide some relevant insights into rural schools in southern Mexico and the variety of educational options available at the junior high level.

In Chapter 4 we follow Anay's move north to Ciudad Juárez in a van contracted by a maquiladora to bring employees from the south to fill its assembly lines. This is where Anay met and married Enrique and their family began. Coming out of that time and her early years were dark accounts of several abusive experiences that Anay had suffered in her childhood. Information about familial abuse is provided in the Interpretive Context section to help situate that experience for Anay, and sadly, so many other girls and women around the globe.

Chapter 5 discusses Anay's secondary education. Over the years that I knew her, Anay managed to get a degree in cosmetology, two junior high degrees, and one high school degree while raising four young children. All of these experiences were alternative, and rather creative, approaches to achieving her dream. We provide a little context from other high school students in Anay's program, as well as some general information about secondary education in Ciudad Juárez.

Anay and Enrique were among the thousands of Mexicans who relocated to the border to work in the maquiladoras. In chapter 6, we see the maquiladora work experience from the points of view of Anay, Enrique, and some of their family and friends. Anay and Enrique lived in Ciudad Juárez during the years of the notorious Maquiladora Murders. They also lived through the escalation of violence and murder to alarming rates in 2009. They and their friends were recipients of this violence more than once.

Chapter 7 chronicles Anay and her family's departure from Ciudad Juárez. First they were invited to stay with church friends in Buffalo Gap, Texas, on a visitor's visa for two stays of six months each. When those visas expired, the church group sponsored their move to southern Mexico to begin a missionary program. The Interpretive Context section examines the mass exodus of people from the city during 2009 and 2010.

In chapter 8, Anay and the family are living in southern Mexico, and Anay has opened a school for women. As we conclude, we see how Anay drew upon her agency and her social capital to negotiate an education and to create opportunities for others while living through her difficult experiences in labor and violence.

In early 2012, Anay's brother was killed in the drug-related violence in Ciudad Juárez. Anay's account of this provides a somber epilogue to the book. To protect the family's safety, her brother's name and all of the locations mentioned in southern Mexico are pseudonyms.

| TWO |

Childhood in Southern Mexico

nay's family and her experiences as a child are cen-
tered in a village in southern Mexico of about forty
thousand people. In this book, we will call the village Huixpan. In the summer of 2008, Anay and I traveled to
Huixpan to meet her family, friends, and teachers and to learn
more about her childhood and her educational experiences
there.

Huixpan is the economic heart of a region that comprises
scores of very small farming communities. The village sits on
the narrow slope between the Sierra Madre Mountains and the
Pacific Ocean. A venous network of rivers, too numerous to document on the official map, moves the tumultuous waters of the
mountains to the ocean. The waters defy their banks and nour-
ish the fertile and swampy land. Our visit was in July, the rainy
season, or, as they say, *"el tiempo de la lluvia,"* the time of the
rains. This season is the region's unpredictable god, bringing life
and wonder along with death and destruction. Many conversations are sprinkled with phrases about the ways in which lives
are modified to accommodate this time when the rains fall. The
beekeepers rob the honey early because their bees won't tackle
the heavy wet air but stay in the hive running at a lazy buzz. The
government forbids commercial fishing so the tuna can reproduce in peace. Towns provide covered halls ready to host out-

door events that must suddenly move indoors to avoid being rained out. The fruit harvest sends a feeling of abundance. People congregate, also at a lazy buzz, in the town centers on clear evenings. Annually, when the rains fall, weather reports across the globe periodically show footage of deadly flooding in this part of the world.

One of the nearby communities is now a ghost town because the flood of 1998 brought the side of one of the mountains down the river with it. The mud covered the town and all the houses. Now you can drive through and see only one or two feet of the tops and roofs of the houses above the ground. The federal government provided assistance to the community and funded the construction of many new concrete-block houses a few meters down the road. The front wall of each new little house was painted a coral peach color, and the rest of the walls were gray concrete block. The village where Anay's grandparents lived missed this mud burial, but any village on that slope between the mountains and the sea is subject to brutal flooding and mudslides.

We were stationed in Huixpan in a little motel of ten rooms. Anay recognized the tiny toothless woman who mopped the constant tramp of muddy steps from the white tile walkway, took our money, and gave us towels. Anay greeted her most respectfully and mentioned her grandfather's name. The little woman knew him and returned the warm greeting, "*Que le vaya bien*," the common phrase that means something like, "May it go well with you." We had a friend for the rest of the stay. The room had two beds, a bathroom with a shower, and, oh blessed machine, an air conditioner! I paid twenty-five U.S. dollars per night and could pay five dollars more if we wanted hot water in the shower. No need as we were bathed in steam all day.

When the sun set, the sultry village cooled off a little, and most residents stopped their daily tasks and oozed outside, hoping to catch a cool breeze. The rain was heavy for about two hours in the late afternoon, then drizzled and stopped by evening. This night, the streets quickly filled with people walking or riding by *triciclo*—an adult-sized tricycle with a driver in the back and a seat and an awning up front. We joined them in this migration toward the town centers, taking advantage of the *triciclo* for less than two dollars. Loud music from an electric organ, accompanied by an off-key, also loud voice, came from the open-air restaurant by our hotel. Some cars and many pickups competed with us for space on the road so that we had to dodge and jump a little, but our *triciclo* had ample access to the streets. The plaster houses, painted in a random scatter using all the colors you would find in a twenty-four box of Crayolas, formed a wall down the block, interrupted by small doorways and barred windows.

Several of these homes were converted to accommodate small businesses that the families set up in their front rooms. A family might widen the doorways to provide an open store front and move the living quarters farther to the back. I entered one of these small grocery store/homes to buy bottled water. The family was watching a soccer game on the television. Grandmother got up to take my money but kept one eye on the game. A tortilla machine filled most of another store. Dough, called *masa*, goes through rollers to press it, and then it is cut by something like a giant cookie cutter on a rotating drum and packaged in waxed butcher paper. Modern women in Huixpan and other parts of Mexico can now buy freshly prepared tortillas instead of spending hours mixing, rolling, and patting each one for their families. The store sold nothing but corn tortillas by the kilogram. Another little storefront was a cybercafe where we stopped later to use the computer and Internet—fifty cents per hour.

Anay's cousin Noemi met us there in the plaza. When Anay was a child, if the weather was bad, she could not get home to the *ranchito* in the evenings from Huixpan, so she stayed with Uncle Lalo's family; thus she and Noemi grew to be as close as sisters. Lalo is still her favorite uncle. Noemi, then twenty-three, is well known in the town for her beauty. Anay told me that many people ask why she is not married. She jokes that she's holding out for a husband like Anay's. Noemi still lives in the family home—

the rooms behind their successful market. Like the other markets, this one occupies the front rooms of the house, but Uncle Lalo had to convert several rooms to accommodate their stock of clothing and groceries, and then he extended bedrooms and a kitchen toward the back. Neighbors sit in the molded plastic tables and chairs on the sidewalk out front to have a cold soda and visit in the late afternoon shade. We spent a few evenings there also. Noemi's mother, Alicia, raises chickens in the back. I saw a neighbor stop by to visit a little while, then go inside with Alicia, and a few minutes later walk away with two newly killed chickens dangling by their feet. One day, we got to eat one of Alicia's chickens cooked in *mole*—a traditional Mexican sauce that is a rich blend of chocolate, *chiles*, and spices.

Lalo also owns a small clothing store near the railroad tracks, and Noemi's career is to manage that little store. Noemi tools around town on her misty green motor scooter, modeling her clothing—modern and form-fitting jeans, bejeweled tee shirts, and bright hoop earrings. A disconnect is obvious as all of the other women in the family dress in the "evangelical" style with long, polyester skirts in muted shades of gray and brown, formless blouses, long hair, and no makeup. But when I saw their prideful admiration of this beautiful daughter, I understood why they couldn't clip her wings too closely.

In my conversations with Mexicans, I often hear them refer to religions in two categories—*católicos* (Catholics) and *cristianos* (Christians). The protestant groups are lumped together as Christian. Catholicism still dominates in Mexico, but in these southern Mexican states, Protestant and evangelical groups are evident, with more than 15 percent of the population converted as a result of a strong effort by missionaries from the United States in the 1960s (Kahn, 2002). Some of the Catholic efforts are wrapped in liberation theology and the rights of indigenous groups. In Huixpan, I saw a Catholic church in one of the plazas and a few small evangelical churches on some side streets. Even in the rural villages of only a few families that we visited, there was a Catholic church and two tiny evangelical churches of slightly different brands.

UNCLE MARGARITO'S CAFÉ

"My name, Anay, I think really that my name should not be pronounced 'an eye' [she pointed to her eye] but 'an aja.' It's a Mayan name. My Uncle Margarito gave me my name. When he was a young man, a Mayan girl—young, maybe fourteen—came down from the mountains to sell fruit in Huixpan. He said she was very beautiful, and they fell in love. He wanted to marry her, and she stayed in Huixpan with him a few days. One night, the men from her tribe in the mountains came down and stole her. They took her back to the mountains. One month later, they brought her back to my uncle. She was dead. He said he never found a mark on her body, so he doesn't know how she died. Her name was Anay. I love my Uncle Margarito. But I think his wife does not like me very much for this story of how I got my name."

We visited Uncle Margarito that night. There are two plazas, two hearts for Huixpan. They are distinguished as the plaza by the railroad tracks and the plaza by the municipal offices. Uncle Margarito owns a little café and mini convenience store located on the second, newer plaza by the municipal offices. As the night wore on, more and more young people came to this plaza, to shop in the stores that stayed open late, to mingle, and to eat in the café, which is famous in the area for its Huixpan Hot Dogs. Uncle Margarito invented them—wieners wrapped in ham, then bacon, placed in a bun, and finally sprinkled with shredded chicken and topped with mayonnaise and chopped tomato. They sell for twelve pesos, about a dollar. I wasn't sure if I could tackle this mound of multiple meats, but I had to try it. The good news is that all over Mexico, you are never more than a few meters away from a large bottle of wonderful liquid hot sauce called Valentina. The kids squirted a healthy stream of catsup (in Spanish, the correct pronunciation is "cat soup") down the middle and then sprinkled Valentina liberally over it all. I skipped the cat soup, loaded on the hot sauce, ordered an extra soda, and wolfed it down.

The plaza and the café were full, and Anay and Noemi

joined their uncle and cousins in making and serving the hot dogs. They sold fifty hot dogs per hour during the busiest time. I sat at my table and observed the young friends talking and laughing.

In this small town, families and friendships run deep and wide. It was a reunion for Anay.

"Oh, Karla! Look at you! You are still with Herman? You got married! You didn't write me! So, what are you doing now? Me? Oh, I have four children. You think so? I think I am a little fat. I just don't eat much anymore."

"No, I don't have a northern accent, do I? It's only been ten years since I moved there. I'll have to get back my southern accent."

"Concha, did you finish your school? No! You should go back. I am about to graduate from high school. Yes! With four little kids! So, you can do it too!"

Later that night, Anay hugged me very tightly and said, "Mommy,[1] tonight was a beautiful therapy. I got to help my Uncle Margarito, and I got to be with Noemi, and I got to see my old friends. And tomorrow we will go see my grandparents!"

THE *RANCHITO*

Sometime in the 1990s, the road was built over the four and a half miles between Huixpan and the tiny village where Anay's grandparents' *ranchito* was located. It was built by adding enough dirt and rocks to elevate a track over the swampy land. The second morning of our visit, Anay's fourteen-year-old cousin, Daniel, drove us on that road to the *ranchito* in Uncle Lalo's '76 Chevy pickup truck with side rails welded over the bed. We drove (more like crept) over the very rocky road, a trip that took almost an hour. The slow pace allowed me to examine nature in her abundance in this tropical land. I couldn't capture the names of the many plants and birds that Anay and Daniel ticked off along the way. I remember horses standing in water almost to their bellies eating the swampy grasses. Little *ranchitos* dotted the few areas where the land was higher than the water.

When we arrived at the *ranchito*, several children ran to greet us. Grandmother Eva fought to the front of the crowd and grabbed Anay in a strong hug. I was behind Anay, so I saw Eva's hands, one grasping the back of Anay's head and the back of the other hand wiping the rain of emotions from her eyes and her nose. She pushed Anay back, cupped her face, kissed her eyes and lips, and hugged her again and harder. Anay laughed and moved to hug Grandfather Francisco, whose wide smile made his long gray mustache meet up with his fuzzy gray sideburns. I got the Mexican polite handshakes with a cheek touch, air kiss.

The water made the *ranchito* a paradise to my desert eyes. We were about a mile from the ocean, and at one with the river that ran a few yards from the *ranchito*. Fresh fish are so abundant that they are considered food for the common people—nothing you would serve a special guest.

The young cousins who lived next door to Grandmother Eva were fascinated with the big *americana*.[2] They delighted in showing me all the fruits that grow on the *ranchitos*—mostly fruits I had never seen or heard about. There was rambutan—a delicious plumlike fruit whose shell is a red, hairy ball. The older cousin showed me how to squeeze one end of the fruit tightly between my thumb and the crook of my first finger until the peel cracks open on the top. The first time I squeezed too hard and the sweet meat of the fruit shot across the table. The children snickered at first, not knowing if laughing would be rude, but they couldn't hold it, and I soon had four young teachers doubled over with laughter trying to show me how to squeeze it just right. With a little practice I could catch the crack in the peel at the right time to open it with my fingers. I recognized some of these fruits—pineapple, mandarin oranges, coconut, grapefruit, and *guayaba* (guava). New to me were delicious fruits with juicy names like *carambola, guanábana, chico zapote,* and *nanze*. Anay's favorite is the coconut, so she asked the little cousins to climb up a tree and bring her one. One of the boys crawled barefoot up the tree and threw the coconut down to the other kids, who ran it to Grandmother. Grandmother Eva grabbed the machete and whacked off the top. She poured the juice into a glass for Anay and me. Anay scraped out the coconut meat to eat with the milk.

As if they were part of our party, hens and little chicks shared the shade with us, scratching in the mud for a treat, dashing to catch a crumb from the table, and dodging big feet. There were not only white chickens but the ones that I have seen in the state fairs, big red hens and roosters and those black and white spotted ones. And this was our lunch: chicken-from-the-ranch soup, cage free and chemical free. The chicken chunks in the soup were not cut at the joints as we cut chicken, but chopped in pieces across the bone an inch or two long. I wondered how they cut it that way, until I saw Grandmother whack that top off of the coconut with her machete. Then I knew.

The house on the *ranchito* consists of three rustic buildings. The original building was the one Anay grew up in. Four large tree trunks were buried in the hard mud to form the four corners of the house. The roof was made of palm leaves layered about a foot thick. I asked Grandfather if he had made the roof. Yes, he had made this one about twenty-five years before. It took him about a week to make it. The sides of the house were rough planks of wood. There was a door opening but no door. The main and original building was the kitchen area. Inside it was a well with a rope, one end of which was wound over a horizontal post with a hand crank and the other tied to a bucket. Our chicken-from-the-ranch soup was cooking over an open fire on an iron grate set on a concrete base. There was also a wooden table and a concrete stand with a version of a sink. A small room had been added onto the back of this building, and the doorway to the room had a curtain over it. Inside was a modern toilet that drained into a septic tank. Anay had to show me how to flush it. There was a bucket of water nearby, and we poured a gallon or two of water into the bowl. The water went on down just fine.

The sink was a sturdy table with a concrete top that had two recessed areas. The recessed areas sloped to an opening where water could drain off. A bucket of water sat to one side. Anay's Aunt Rosie, the mother of the little cousins who showed me the fruit, was helping Grandmother Eva with the meal. Rosie dipped a plastic bowl in the water bucket, grabbed a pinch of powdered soap, and washed her hands with water poured from the plastic bowl. In a similar manner, they wash dishes and clothes at this sturdy sink. There was no running water in the *ranchitos* or the houses I visited in Huixpan, and this form of sink was common. Other than the need to bring a heavy bucket of water to the sink every morning and the inconvenience of not having instant hot water, the system without running water worked well.

Anay and Grandmother led me through the home. There were two other buildings built similarly with palm roofs. A table and a wooden frame bed with rope webbing were inside one of the buildings. "This was my bed when I was little," claimed Anay. Looking down at it, she shook her head. "Better beds today!" The third building was for storage. There were no doors or locks on any of these palm-roof buildings. On this *ranchito*, Francisco and Eva raised twelve sons, one of their two daughters, and Anay.

In 1998, the rains brought a great flood to this part of Mexico. One of the cousins showed me a mark on the wall of the house that indicated the height of the floodwater—over four feet. They did have some advance warning; Cousin Daniel said that his brothers waded through the waters to find all of the chickens and get them to the road. Aunt Rosie and her family had a pickup truck, so they packed it full and left before the flood came. No lives were lost, but much was destroyed. The government aided the people by building small houses out of concrete block with two small rooms, each about eight feet by eight feet. Every family in this tiny community where the *ranchito* is located now has one of the block houses.

In that tropical land, catching a breeze is more important than having solid walls of block, so almost all the residents repaired their palm-top open houses and continued to live in them, and they used the new block houses with doors

to store valuables. It was common to see families sitting outside of the block house, peering through the open door at the
television that was inside. The day we spent with Grandmother
and Grandfather, Anay and I never went inside the block house.
Everyone wore sandals to walk on the cool, packed earth. But I
noticed that when Grandmother came to the concrete floor of
the block house, she left her sandals outside and entered barefoot. In spite of the greater coolness of the palm-topped house, a
house of block seemed to bring more status.

According to Anay, when a family in this area lives in a
nicer house or has a good car, it is likely that the husband works
on *el otro lado*, the other side (common term for the United
States). Here in southern Mexico, many men have left and found
work in the fields or meat processing plants in the United States.
A few of them find new lives and new families far away on the
other side, and they either abandon their families in Mexico or
just take on a second family, each hidden from the other.

Aunt Rosie lives next door to Eva and Francisco. She has a
pickup truck, a block house, the palm-top extension, and some
nice furniture. Her husband, Eva's youngest son, works in an
agriculture-related job in New Jersey. No one could tell me what
town or what job other than working in the fields. She has a cell
phone, and the ring tone plays a ballad from a popular Mexican
band moaning about being alone in the United States and missing the family at home.

The last time Rosie saw her husband was three years ago,
when he came home for a visit. He left Rosie pregnant with her
fifth child. The baby, about two, still nursed at Rosie's breast—
now long and flat after five babies. About every hour she
climbed up in Rosie's lap and lifted Rosie's shirt to nurse. She
still had princess status and strutted around in her little sandals that squeaked when she walked. Grandmother Eva lifted
her high above her head, which seemed a very young move for
a seventy-one-year-old, little, bent, gray grandmother, and sang
a little song to her. "Ling-a-ling-a-ling-ling. Ling-a-ling-a-ling-
ling." She glanced toward Anay and muttered, "That's what I
sang when *you* were a baby." I don't think Anay heard her.

Rosie's older daughter and three sons had been demoted from the limelight with the arrival of the new baby, but Grandmother Eva still called them each by name, joked with them, hugged them, and teased them. They stayed with us the whole day, visiting politely.

After lunch Grandfather Francisco, Grandmother Eva, Anay, Cousin Daniel, Rosie, Rosie's children, and I sat around the table for *sobremesa*. This is one of my favorite parts of Mexican life: you sit around the table with a full stomach, all relaxed, and talk about your history, your day, and your dreams. Grandmother Eva is half Zapotec Indian with a profile like those classic Mayan figures carved in the ancient stones. Anay asked her to tell me about her childhood. Eva flitted from task to task and idea to idea. She wouldn't concentrate more than a few seconds, so we only got snippets of the story. She started by declaring that she was not Zapotec.

Anay said, "Yes, grandmother, you are. You spoke the Zapotec language when you were married, and your mother is full Zapotec. It is okay to be Indian. It is not bad now."

When Grandmother Eva walked away, Anay turned to me and spoke softly. "Grandmother has told me this story many times. When she was fourteen, her family sold her to an older man to be his wife. He was always beating her. She could remember hiding up in a hayloft one night. He was drunk and came after her with a sharp stick. He poked and poked at her through the hay. She was in a corner higher up, so he didn't get her. She waited until he fell asleep, and she ran away that very night and hid outside her parents' home. She said she would never go back to that man. They were mad at her because he had a lot of money. Soon she started living with a teacher."

"Grandfather left home when he was twelve. His parents didn't care for him at all. He just lived in the fields. When he met Eva, he robbed her from the teacher, and now they have been married for more than fifty years. When Grandmother was young, she worked in a bar. She started drinking then and was alcoholic for most of her life."

Almost 25 percent of the citizens in this area are members

of indigenous groups. Colonial and exploitive practices often cause them to be seen as defeated, marginal groups. So some rural people denounce their indigenous roots.[3]

The young cousins wanted to practice English with the *americana*. One ran next door to his house and brought me a book. It was an elementary history text written in English. I know that language development is built in relevant concepts, and the dry succession of presidents of the United States was probably not the way to learn this new language. So we talked about food like hot dogs and pizza. We practiced counting in English. And I taught them common greetings like "Hey!" "Hi!" and "High five." We all practiced high fives. Grandmother Eva joined in and greeted the little cousin with a high five, (and a pretty rough pronunciation of the phrase).

The usually quiet Grandfather muttered, "What was that? A new kind of Zapotec?"

Soon the cousins perked up and said, "It's the teacher. He's here to cut the tree." The boys jumped up to help with the task, and Anay went off to visit her old teacher and to join the action. I stayed with Grandmother Eva sitting at the table in the shade while the others were busy with the tree cutting.

Grandmother Eva brought a new-looking Bible out from the block house. I started writing in my notebook. Eva spread the Bible on the table and smoothed out the pages. Eva had only a few years of schooling, but there was quite a show of taking off and putting on glasses, smoothing the tissue-like pages, running a finger down the columns of numbered verses, and muttering affirmative syllables. She flitted some more. She grabbed my ring and commented on it. With a hissing sound she shooed a dog who was trying to enter the block house. He retreated. She muttered to the hen and chickens nearby and shooed flies from the table. "There are so many flies because the rains are falling now." She muttered something about fifty-two years she has been married. She spat a stream of orders to Grandfather to be careful with that saw, to move the truck out of the way, to take his good shirt off, to stack the wood just so, and to cut the dead wood. The saw was buzzing, and he could not have heard any of the orders, but they kept coming. Then, more muttering while she ran her finger down the column and turned the page in her Bible.

After the visit to the *ranchito*, Cousin Daniel drove us back to Huixpan. On the way, I discovered how the rural bus system works. If a man owns a pickup or slightly larger truck, he can modify the bed of the truck by adding side rails and maybe an awning. He can now become a bus driver. Apparently, this is an organized system because the "buses" run on a somewhat regular schedule. If you live in a *ranchito* and want to go to town, you walk out to the road and wait for the bus. The driver will pause for you to jump in the back. We saw drivers stop to help the elderly folks get in, or maybe let them ride up front if they could not climb into the back. Then, when you are close to your destination in town, you knock on the cab of the truck. The driver will stop for you to get down and pay. Rides cost from a quarter to a few dollars, depending on the distance. However, if someone like Daniel comes by in his pickup, you can flag him down, and he'll give you a ride for free. We had three passengers by the time we returned to Huixpan.

Early in the morning of the next day of our visit to her childhood home, Anay and I walked to the plaza to get a cup of coffee. Huixpan is not far from a region called Huehuetenango. The coffee from this area is well known, and perhaps my favorite. Coffee trees were abundant on the hillside. I wrapped my tongue around the melodic Huehuetenango and expected a coffee experience. We walked most of a mile to a little café on the plaza for the only coffee one could buy in Huixpan—instant Nescafé. (Coffee is grown in the region, but the raw beans are exported. The value of exporting the beans exceeds the demand for gourmet coffee in a small Mexican town.) That became our morning ritual. It grew on me, and I drink Nescafé most mornings now. On our walk to the plaza, Anay talked.

"There, that's the house I was born in, right there beside my Uncle Lalo's store. That's where the midwife lived. My baby hair was golden. My grandmother went up and down the streets asking if they wanted me, the little golden baby. Many women said, yes, they would like the baby, but, no, they did not have money to pay the midwife. So, I just stayed at the house with the midwife for several days. She wouldn't let me go until someone paid her fees. Finally, when no one could pay, the midwife told Grandmother Eva to just take me and pay her some money whenever she could. So Grandmother wrapped me in a towel and got up on the horse. She rode back to the *ranchito*, and I lived with her until I was thirteen."

She looked down at her shoes and stopped talking, lost in thought. After a few minutes, she spoke again.

"I don't like to talk about my birth. It is a little painful. My mother was so young, and she could not love a baby. And Grandmother wouldn't let her. It was hard. I still love my grandmother.

"My father was the young teacher. My mother said he wanted to marry my mother, but she was only fourteen, and he didn't have any money, and Grandfather wouldn't permit it. The teacher left town and never returned. My mother was living with another man who was nice and took her in, but I'm sure my father was the teacher. Some people here know where he is now. Maybe someday I can go find him. My mother just wanted to get away from Grandmother Eva, I'm sure. So, after I was born, she lived with the old man, Don Arturo. He is as old as my grandfather. They are still together today. He's the one that hurt me that way, you know.

"I walked these streets with Grandfather selling fish when I was very young, oh, maybe four years old. I could balance the basket of fish on my head. Those were fun memories with Grandfather. When we had a little money, we had the horse, and we would ride to town on the horse. Unless it was flooding! Then we had to walk it and hold our clothes in a plastic bag over our heads. That took hours! I was so scared that I would wash away. Those floods were bad memories.

"But, when I got older, yes, every year that I was in elementary school, I had to sell in the streets every day after school from first grade through sixth grade—every day! Grandmother went with me when I was young. But when I was about nine, I had to sell by myself. Some days Grandfather's fish, most of the time fruit and *nuegados*. After school, I would go to Grand-mother's kitchen and she gave me a big basket to sell. I put it on my head and walked to Huixpan on one day, then to Padilla one day, and Villa Paz one day—any of the little villages around. We didn't get home until it was dark and I still had to do my stud-ies. We had these lamps—you would put oil in a glass bottle and stuff a rag in there and light that. That is how I read my books in the night.

"If I didn't sell the whole basket, Grandmother beat me. I had marks on my arms and legs. I think the people knew this, because usually they would all buy the fruit or the *nuegados*, so most of the time I did sell everything. She could still beat me! Usually when she was drunk. She was an alcoholic then. She doesn't drink now. I think she is sorry for what she did.

"One time, when she was drunk, she wanted to go to an-other village to get more beer. She made me go with her on the horse. I was only about four years old. It was night. She fell asleep on the horse and then slid off. We were in the middle of the forest. I didn't know what to do, so I slid down and crouched down beside her. I couldn't wake her. That horse stayed right be-side me. I think he knew I was afraid. I heard the animals in the forest howling. I was so scared. All night I stayed frozen in that spot praying to God, 'Please don't let the animals eat me. Please don't let the animals eat me.' Finally, when the sun was coming up, some men came by the place where we were. They were go-ing to check on their cattle. They found me and woke up Grand-mother and sent us home. I was so scared that bad night. I still have nightmares about it."

I checked the map. One of the villages where Anay walked to sell the produce is over two miles away from the *ranchito*, and Huixpan is well over four miles. One trip could take up to four hours.

Grandmother Eva's *nuegados* seemed to be famous in Huix-pan. She made some for us while we were there. She mixed up her secret recipe of flour, sugar, and a little fruit juice. Then, she rolled the dough in little balls less than an inch in diameter. Anay was helping, and Eva corrected her often to get the balls to exactly the right size. She invited me to help. When we finished, I walked over to examine the nearby well. Out of the corner of my eye, I saw her glance my way, and then subtly re-roll a few of my dough balls. Then she fried them in hot oil. While still hot, she rolled them in a sugar syrup she made in a skillet. When I finally got to taste one, it was something between food for the goddesses and the best Krispy Kreme donut hole you ever tasted. Anay said, "She taught me how to make *nuegados*, but I can never get it right. I can't remember the recipe." Grandmother gave Anay a bagful to take to her family back in Ciudad Juárez. Anay placed the bag in the refrigerator for safekeeping while we visited. When we departed, she left the bag of *nuegados* in Grandmother's refrigerator. I started to remind her to get the bag, and then I thought, perhaps in forgetting the *nuegados* Anay was trying to avoid remembering.

THE OTHER LITTLE STREET VENDOR

Having deep and sustained conversations with a busy mother of four is difficult. The moments with Anay during our trip to southern Mexico were precious, and I planned a relaxed time to visit—one whole day where we were together with no children, no relatives, and no teachers. Cousin Jairo drove us to a little seaside community with only two hotels. We selected one, but Jairo wouldn't let us out of his pickup until he talked to the owners and was convinced that they were honest people. They passed his test, and we sent him off with hugs and warm wishes to his generous family. Our little room did have an air conditioner, which produced large quantities of noise and small quantities of cool air. We gathered our beach gear, flagged down a pickup "taxi," and rode to the beach.

Several small restaurateurs had set up shop in this beach community—each with a small kitchen and eating area to which was added a large palm-roof shade, called a *palapa*, that extended over the sand toward the beach. Plastic tables and chairs, along with string hammocks, were set up in the shade of the *palapas*. We were allowed to sit under the *palapa* all day as long as we ordered some food or drink from the restaurant. Since we arrived earlier than the crowd that Sunday morning, we staked out the best table for beach and hammock access. Mexican music, always loud and almost always from bad speakers, sprinkled with some Christian songs in Spanish, filled the air space. The weather was perfect. When the sun was high overhead, the sand was so hot that you had to find the most direct line from the *palapa*'s shade to your spot in the waves and then dance the run-hop, singing, "Ouch, ouch, ouch!" until you hit the cool mud.

Now, I prefer a Mexican Corona over a sugary soft drink most any time, especially for eighty cents. So I ordered the beer and Anay ordered a soft drink. Anay and the owner opened their eyes widely when I placed my beer order. I was getting the feeling that women don't drink beer in public much, at least not at ten in the morning in that small community. Anay said that a beer and an ankle bracelet were cultural signs for hookers. I was halfway there. Before long, that Corona and Anay's beauty attracted a couple of men. They moved to the table next to ours, and one of them plopped down in the hammock assigned to our table. They spoke a little English, and maybe they just wanted to visit and practice. But I was not going to give up my precious moments with Anay. The restaurant owner must have felt that he needed to take good care of us, because he showed up and asked loudly, "Is everything okay here?," trying to hint to the men to move along. We assured him we were fine, but as soon as we had a chance, we relocated to a less visible table. Throughout the day, people moved in and out, and before long we were back at our special beachside table with the hammock.

We were wearing shorts and tee shirts, as were all the bathers. I saw no swimsuits. Several tee shirts had messages in English that caught my eye. One man's shirt said, "My son whacked your honor student and now he is stupid." And a little grandmother sported one with a downward arrow under the words, "There's a bun in the oven." One grandfather was dozing in a hammock with a baby fast asleep on top of his ample stomach. Families greeted us warmly, and we exchanged short greetings.

Anay and I took turns in our hammock, talked, and soaked up the peaceful atmosphere.

Anay befriended many of the families playing in the shallow waters. So we visited and swam and helped teach a few children how to float. We returned to our table under the palm shade for a snack and a rest. A constant stream of local vendors weaved in and out among the vacationers. A woman carrying a large bag stopped at our table. She pulled out several hand-embroidered dresses—cool and comfortable for warm climates. A bent little man pushed his cart of *raspas*—a kind of snow cone. He scraped ice from a block into a paper cup and poured over it our choice of mango or tamarind juice. Other vendors streamed by selling items such as beaded necklaces, sunglasses, small plastic toys, and shrimp cocktails. Anay visited politely and respectfully with all of the vendors. If we were just not interested at all, we gave the Mexican code phrase for "No," which is, "*No hoy, gracias*," which translates to, "Not today, thank you." I have found that the vendors will stay with you giving sales talks no matter how you protest; but as soon as you utter that polite phrase, they move along.

One vendor was a young girl with a round face that showed her Mayan heritage. She walked to our table with a basket of fruit—watermelon, pineapple, and papaya sprinkled with *chile* powder—balanced on her head. Anay stopped her and hopped up. "What is your name, sweetheart? Did you know that I used to sell fruit with a basket on my head, just like you? May I?" And she took the girl's basket, balanced it on her head, and walked around our table. "See, I can still do it. Now, what are you selling?"

The girl set the basket on our table and spoke to us with a confident air. She said that she was eleven years old and her name was Jessica. "I am here with my grandfather and grandmother. Grandfather is over there. He has the cart selling the *raspas*. Grandmother helps him when she can. But she has diabetes and her heart is so weak. All the pills and the doctor's bills . . . I don't know what we'll do with her. Every morning she is so tired. She fixes the fruits. But her legs hurt and her eyes are going bad. Oh my, it is such a difficult time."

I could picture little Jessica hearing this speech from her aching grandmother every morning and parroting it back to us. As we selected our fruit from her basket, she asked where we were from. Anay told her that she was from right here, and now she lived in Juárez and had just finished high school. "Are you going to school?" Jessica nodded. "Good. You can finish high school also. It is very important."

When I told her that I was from the United States, her eyes lit up.

"I have adoptive parents in the United States. They send me presents for my birthday and for Christmas. Well, not really presents. I tell the church people what present I want, and they send the money. Then the church people buy the present. See my pretty bracelets? They bought those for my birthday when I was eleven. And they send me a card with the presents."

"Yes, the bracelets are beautiful. Have you ever met your adoptive parents?" I asked as I admired the collection of small beaded bracelets on her arm.

"No, it is just through the church people. They have my picture, and sometimes they send me a letter. It's in English, but the church people help me read it."

This arrangement sounded much like Save the Children and similar charities advertised in the United States. You select a child in a high-poverty area of the world. You receive the child's picture and a little biography if you commit to send a small amount of money regularly to provide food and gifts for them. To Jessica, this arrangement was a great source of pride.

Jessica went on to sell her fruit, but she made a swing by our table every few minutes. When her basket was empty, she sat down with us. "Do you know how to swim?" she asked. "Good. Would you take me swimming?" So we entered the warm, gentle waters of the bay. Anay asked her if she could float, and demonstrated. Jessica said no, so we got on each side of her and held her up while she got her balance and soon took off floating.

Then I heard, in English, "My turn." I turned around to see a little boy with short, spiky hair, about the same age as Jessica, smile and lie back in our arms for a floating lesson. As his body came out of the water, I hid my surprise to see bikini bottoms and budding breasts. She said her name was Margarita. Margarita learned to float as quickly as Jessica. I spoke to her in English, but she did not understand much. It is still a mystery where she learned "My turn."

Then both girls took off swimming like dolphins! They had just wanted the attention, and feigning the need for swim lessons was a door into our day. So we spent happy hours conducting swimming races and building sand castles.

Anay asked Margarita, "Who cut your hair?"

She answered, "My dad. I was being punished because I had head lice. I don't have a mom."

Some folks from the families playing in the waves came close to us and began practicing their English words. We bobbed in the waves and discussed a range of topics from languages to foods to politics and presidents.

Later, Anay and I were on our own again. We swam out to the middle of the bay. None of the other vacationers ventured out this far. The water was so salty that we were very buoyant. We could tread water with ease. On my toes, I could feel the cool water of the river flowing out to the ocean. The upper layer of water was still, warm, and salty. We talked in this relaxing bath for a long time.

"Sometimes I would stay at my mother's house for a weekend. When I returned, Grandmother had to get the lice out of my hair. She would get some of the course sand from the seashore. Then she parted my hair in thin sections. She rubbed the sand on the roots. She rubbed hard, but she didn't try to hurt me. Then she combed the hair with those combs with the tiny teeth. Then she did the same thing, but the second time, she used wet sand. Then she rinsed it out with lots of water and combed it and combed it with the thin combs. Sometimes, if you got lice, they just shaved all your hair off. Grandmother never did that."

In addition to the sand treatment, special shampoo to get

rid of the head lice is available in drugstores. Margarita's father selected the humiliating option. The child seemed to be on her own, un-chaperoned at the beach, and now I try not to think about the tender girl and her home experiences.

As the sun began to go down, Jessica joined us for dinner. As Jessica peeled her shrimp, she looked up at us and said, "My mother is in the United States." Then she stopped as tears streamed out of her eyes. Between sobs, she told us, "We don't know where she is. When she left, we never heard from her again." Another child missing her mother's love. This one is complicated with a debilitating unknown. Was Jessica's mother dead from the dangerous crossing experience? Was she in some situation where she was unable to communicate? Or, did she find a new life in the United States?

Anay took over and made the conversation full of comfort as she told events in her own life that were similar to Jessica's. She gave Jessica her phone number and address and said she could call her any time. We finished our meal and joined a group of children who were in the small pool near the back of the palm shade until Jessica's grandmother called for her to help take her grandfather's *raspa* cart home, and we sent her on her way with lots of hugs and kisses.

The two fruit vendors developed a sisterhood through their similar life experiences. Both Anay and Jessica lived with their grandparents and helped provide income by selling fruits out of baskets carried on their heads. Both girls longed for their mothers' love. Almost twenty years later, young girls still sell from baskets on their heads to help provide family resources.

INTERPRETIVE CONTEXT:
CHILD LABOR AND INFORMAL MARKETS

To understand a little more about child labor in Mexico, we will start with an experience back in Ciudad Juárez. During my visits over the years to Ciudad Juárez, I spent many hours in the long line of cars slowly creeping up and over the Rio Grande on the international bridge back into El Paso. The space between the car lanes is a market fair of vendors of all ages, some wearing blue vests to indicate that they had registered with the city, and some not. Vendors offer a wide variety of goods: flavorful Mexican popsicles, fresh fruit sprinkled with *chile* salt, newspapers and magazines, candy, water, cheap toys, handcrafted musical instruments, and scores of images of the Virgin of Guadalupe crafted in a variety of media, including plastic, paper, wood, plaster, and textiles. Other vendors wash your windows, dust your car, or play music for a donation. Many of these vendors are informal, unregistered vendors, outside of the official employment numbers and outside of the tax obligations.

All around the nation, you can see individuals, men and women, old and young, selling anything that someone might buy—foods, toys, pirated music, crafts, animals, shoe shines, and car washes. The vendors are at the stop signs, on the buses, in shopping areas, and along the highways. Informal markets such as these occur all over the world; but in communities or countries where economic resources are scarce, these resourceful and creative activities provide a thin blanket for survival.

This informal economic exchange includes market and service transactions that are conducted unofficially and untaxed. The informal economy accounts for 44 percent of urban jobs in Mexico, moving about $146 billion a year, according to Franco (1999), but *Frontera NorteSur* (2010) cites sources that estimate it at about $76 billion per year. With either estimate, informal sales account for a very large portion of the economic activity in the country, and the amount greatly exceeds the country's income from oil and tourism.

The abundance of informal economic activity is linked to widespread poverty and the lack of social safety nets. The economic changes brought on by Mexico's participation in the North American Free Trade Agreement (NAFTA) reduced agricultural employment in such large numbers that many displaced workers could not find employment in the newly emerging foreign industrial programs. They were pushed into the informal labor sector. "As a result of the 'reforms' . . . almost a third of the

Mexican people have been forced into penurious, petty hustling and scrabbling to eke out an existence on the margins of modernity" (Floyd, 2010).

Women with few financial resources carry out these informal economic activities primarily in the streets or as domestic servants in others' homes. Social status delineates informal employment of women in Mexico. Middle-class women will sell items out of their homes but will not sell in the streets or work in other women's homes. Thus, the women with the fewest resources take on the jobs of street vendors and domestic help. As such, their labor is more intense and they are more vulnerable to abuse (Arizpe, 1997).

Although Mexican law prohibits children under the age of fourteen from working, the United Nations Children's Fund, UNICEF, states that 16 percent of children between the ages of five and fourteen were involved in child labor activities in 2009. These data indicate that approximately 3.6 million Mexican children aged five to seventeen work in agriculture or sales, some in part-time labor and others working many hours per day. About 1.5 million of these working children did not attend school; instead, they worked to augment the family income. Mexican government agencies are active in trying to decrease the number of children who are working; however, that task is most difficult in the informal sector, where most children work (U.S. Department of State, 2009).

Those working in the informal sector are not eligible for the nation's social security or health care. The jobs often involve heavy manual labor, long hours, and exposure to extreme elements. Women often must bring their children along to their jobs, and children who sell in the streets are particularly vulnerable to crime. Going to school becomes a luxury that the family cannot afford. Anay and Jessica were able to work in informal sales and still attend elementary school. But Anay lost her opportunity to attend junior high because her grandmother sent her to work as a domestic in a woman's home. Jessica and Margarita probably face a future in informal labor, most likely at the expense of secondary education.

THREE

Rural School in Southern Mexico

I loved elementary school. In first, second, and third grade I had to walk to Huixpan every day to school. It took about forty-five minutes, and you know my Grandfather did not want me to go alone. So he walked with me to town, then walked home, then walked back to pick me up, and we walked home. That was the first years. In fourth grade the teacher came here. That year, we sat under a tree down the street from Grandmother's *ranchito*. That was our schoolhouse—that mango tree right there! Then, the next year the government built a schoolhouse for us."

Later in her life, the maquiladora industry in Ciudad Juárez sent its long arm into the south and took, first, Anay's mother and, later, Anay to that city. Anay was able to accomplish her goal of a high school education, although many difficulties made that accomplishment a rough and steep climb. The only time when Anay had easy access to education was during three years of her primary education when a school was provided in her grandparents' village.

THE TEACHER ON THE MOTORCYCLE

While Anay and I were visiting her home, I had the opportunity to interview two of her teachers. While we were eating the chicken-from-the-ranch soup, Profe Rogelio[1] came to Grandfather's *ranchito* to help him cut down a tree. After the trees were cut, Anay brought the teacher to the shade to meet me. He was dressed for a hard day's work, with a shirt that was missing most of its buttons and one boot that did not lace shut.

Anay introduced him. "This is Profe Rogelio. He and Profe Nacho were my teachers from first to sixth grade. They came riding their bicycle from Huixpan every day to teach us. One day they had a wreck on the bicycle and Profe Rogelio fell on top of Profe Nacho and broke his arm. We were all mad at Profe Rogelio because he is bigger and Nacho was our favorite, now with a broken arm." She laughed and gave him a nudging kind of hug.

Today, Rogelio still makes that very bumpy trip of four and a half miles every day to teach and help in the community of the *ranchitos*, but nowadays he comes on his motorcycle. He told me the story of the school. This community had no school until about 1995. When Anay was in school, there were about seventy students. The government had a special program for teachers in rural communities. It paid a little extra, close to the equivalent of eighteen hundred U.S. dollars per year, to the teachers to work with the fifteen students who were excelling in school in a special after-school program. In this program the children practiced several subjects and competed in regional contests with other children who were advanced in their schools. This zone included about two hundred schools. "Anay was in our special program. In sixth grade, we took her to one of the competitions. She won every competition for every subject! Even flag ceremony! She won [he ticked off on his fingers] math, and literature, poetry, yes, chess . . . and volleyball. She is still famous in the town for these awards. She was the first girl to win, and the first one to win every competition in one year!"

He spoke with pride and respect about his school that started under a mango tree and is now a two-room, concrete block building. The school population has decreased from seventy to about forty. He explained, "Now there is no work, so the families leave the *ranchitos*." He stood up, wiped sweat from his face with his neck kerchief, and said to me, "So, Profe, this is the story of my school." He turned to Anay and said, "Now, Anayita [little Anay, a term of endearment], I have to go. This summer I am like a farmworker." With polite handshakes all around, he took up his machete and left on his motorcycle.

PROFE NACHO

That night, back in Huixpan, Anay's favorite cousin, Noemi, came on her motor scooter to our hotel to pick up Anay. They were going to visit some friends, including Profe Nacho, the short name for Ignacio. They politely invited me, but I knew they needed time together, and my energy level was dropping. I went to bed, and Anay and her cousin visited.

During her visit, Noemi arranged for Profe Nacho to join us for (instant) coffee on the plaza. He lived on a side road just off the plaza. The next morning we walked to the plaza and Nacho came walking across the plaza to join us. Mexicans greet each other with that cheek-touch, air kiss, and handshake when they meet and when they leave. This can take quite some time in a large group as each person enters, greets every other person with the traditional way, and then repeats it upon leaving. Living in a Mexican American community, I try to remember this custom and not blast in and start attacking my bulleted to-do list, and I'm trying to train my young family members to follow the respectful tradition. So after the greeting with Profe, we sat down, ordered our Nescafé and cookies, and chatted a little about the weather before I asked him to tell me about the school in the *ranchito* community and Anay's elementary education.

The plaza was not set up for interviews. Informal markets are a vital part of the social structure and the economy of rural Mexico. No Walmart, McDonald's, or Starbucks. In fact, I saw no American businesses on the whole trip. Instead, men with pickup trucks loaded with goods drive through the villages and down the rural roads between villages, selling items that back home I would "run to the store to pick up." They have different ways to announce themselves. Many have speakers on their trucks announcing the products, sometimes an advertising song if it is a commercial product. Sometimes just a loud radio. One truck that sold propane gas had a chain with heavy metal rings dangling from the back of the truck scraping along the pavement. Cousin Jairo sells sweet oranges that he imports from Veracruz. He drives around Huixpan and the nearby *ranchito* communities playing a CD of his own band—a Christian rock band. The villagers know that when they hear this music, they can flag him down and buy a box of oranges. On that early morning, the water truck and a few other trucks went about their business and invaded our interview space.

We had to keep shifting tables to escape the early sun's intensity. And Profe Nacho seemed a little intimidated by the big foreign woman at first. He tilted his head away from me and spoke softly. After several moves and several singing trucks, we found a back corner of the café with shade, and Nacho warmed up a little and spoke directly to me. He told us about his vision for education in Mexico.

"See, this is economic riches [moving a coffee cup to the center of the table], and this is education [moving the sugar shaker alongside the coffee cup]. Now, this [moving the packaged cookies into the group] is honesty and respect, like Don Julio. He lives very humbly, just around the corner there; but everyone knows that he is so honest and trustworthy. He will never be unfair. So, you can have economic riches, but still not be rich, or have respect. You need all three. You must have education to make you complete, so you know what are the important social issues and how to address fairness.

"And, I'm not talking just about knowing how to read and do math. You have to know the social issues, what is happening in our state, in our nation, in our village. And why. They leave that out of education now.

"I was awarded a scholarship for all four years to get a

teaching degree in the capital. I went to the education school for men."

I gasped, "For men? They are segregated?"

"Yes, they are segregated, I think because the students are young adults and have to live away from home. But it was a good education—well rounded. We read the great philosophers and the great historians. And we had good background in science, math, you know. And, yes, classes in pedagogy, teaching, and social services. So, yes, things need to change for teachers and education in this state. We are ignored, without resources. But a teachers' strike only hurts the children if you take away a day from school. I still write letters and petition for more resources to education, but I won't strike during the school year.

"We still have trouble getting education to all the kids here in Huixpan, especially the girls. There are two junior high schools here in Huixpan and one high school. So the kids from the *ranchitos* all have to come into Huixpan to finish their school. Some have to travel more than ten miles one way. So the girls don't come. 'It's too dangerous, or it's too far. Better for you to stay and help mom make tortillas.' I can understand how they feel, but we could do something to get the girls to finish their school—different schedules or going to the *ranchitos* . . . something. Now, they don't have any interest in reading books or learning more or changing their lifestyle or more fairness in the community."

He confirmed Profe Rogelio's comments about Anay. He said he was so glad she was in school now because she was indeed a brilliant girl. That evening, I asked Anay if he had a family.

"Yes, he just married when he started teaching us. He had two little babies. Last night he told us that he is not happy that his wife won't finish her high school degree. He has asked her to, but she just wants to stay in the house. She won't read books, and he loves to read books. I don't think she's very good for him."

Anay went on to tell me about her experiences after elementary school in Huixpan.

"After I graduated from sixth grade, I wanted to go to junior high school so bad! But Grandmother said I had to work. I cried and cried. Profe Nacho came to talk to Grandmother to plead with her to change her mind. He said I could babysit his children for a little money if only I could go to school. He really wanted me to go to school. She said, 'No, I already have a job for her working for Señora Muñoz in Huixpan. She will live with her and be her maid and take care of her.' We couldn't change my grandmother's mind. So, I didn't get to go to school.

"Well, Señora Muñoz was very nice. All of her children had left her and gone to work in America. She was so lonely. Mostly, my job was to listen to her talk about when her husband died, and when her children left, and what her children were doing now. She was always sad and told the same stories over and over. They never came back, but they wrote letters to her. She wanted me to be with her all the time. We got up together and fixed meals together and cleaned the garden together. You can see her house from Uncle Margarito's café. Remember all those big trees in the back? I picked up every leaf, *every leaf* that fell from those trees in her garden. It used to be full of flowers and fruits, with the plants forming patterns. Very beautiful. She never had a car, but she lived so close we just walked to the market. Of course, she never carried the bags home. She said that was my job because I was younger.

"So, I stayed working for her for a year. Then another one of my uncles came to visit from Mexico City. He had four young children. He told Grandmother that I could go live with them and help take care of the children. I could work nearby to pay my share of the food and electric bills. So I went to Mexico City. They were Christians, so I didn't go out anywhere except to their youth activities. I lived there two years and never saw any of the pyramids or museum there. I just spent my time walking to the lady's house where I did all the washing and cleaning and walking back to take care of the kids in the evening. I gave my uncle most of my wages working for this lady and had a little left to buy some clothes and some snacks."

It was about this time that an opportunity to move to Ciudad Juárez held the hope of continuing her education.

INTERPRETIVE CONTEXT:
RURAL SCHOOLING IN MEXICO

Hernán Cortés led the conquest of Mexico in the early 1500s. Soldiers and priests participated in the conquest and supported Cortés's goal of converting the indigenous Mexicans to their version of Christianity. Very quickly, education became the tool for this purpose. In 1529, Frey Pedro de Gante (Villar, 1529) wrote about the earliest schools for the children of the Aztec nobles. The schools taught Spanish language, reading, and writing in the daytime and religious doctrine at night. The best students were selected to be trained as evangelists so that they could reach into the Aztec villages and assist in the conversion of these Indians to Catholicism. These special students were allowed to keep their native Aztec languages for the purpose of evangelizing the indigenous Aztecs. Thus, Mexican education has a long history shrouded in a specific purpose, designed to advance religious and civil domination.

Less than one-third of Mexicans now live in rural areas, but this population is scattered in small communities, often in remote locations, thus compounding the difficulties of rural education in the nation. Few teachers will travel the rutted and dangerous roads to these remote locations, and few in the rural communities have specialized training to prepare educators. Many children have to travel several miles, and some families cannot invest the time and money needed for this commute. Since these communities are often agriculture based, the children have family responsibilities that may prevent their school participation. And, often, the families feel it is acceptable for boys to walk a mile or two to school but are reluctant to send their girls on these long trips alone. These challenges to education in rural areas are not unique to Mexico; they occur in most any developing country.

Fortunately, Anay was able to attend a publicly funded school in Grandmother's village. Her teachers had to travel about one hour each way on the undeveloped road. Funding for a building came, slowly, as a result of Profe Nacho's persistent requests. The teachers were paid, and there was additional funding for the zone competitions. Thus, Anay had a relatively strong elementary program, and the teachers and her grandfather helped her overcome obstacles to accessing this education.

Because of a strong government initiative for education in the 1990s, schooling in Mexico is now compulsory through ninth grade, although that mandate is met less often in rural areas for some of the reasons described above. This education is free, and a national curriculum project provides free textbooks to every student in the compulsory programs. However, although the education is free, expenses for uniforms, supplies, and transportation, along with test fees and parent organization fees, may prevent participation.

Even with a strong desire to raise one's educational level, sometimes the incline is too steep. One example illustrates that point. I met Laura and her family in a rural community on the outskirts of Ciudad Juárez when she was in sixth grade. Laura wanted to go to junior high, but her mother did not have the money, so she stayed home one year after finishing sixth grade. Some friends from the United States provided money to pay her registration fee and to buy her uniform to enter the following year. She went for one semester, but ongoing small fees, the long walk to the school (about a mile and a half), and the social and educational impact of missing one year overwhelmed Laura and she dropped out.

Education, across the globe, is embedded in social, economic, and political context. As Richard Shaull says in his introduction to Paolo Freire's *Pedagogy of the Oppressed*,

> There is no such thing as a *neutral* educational process. Education either functions as an instrument that is used to facilitate the integration of the younger generation into the logic of the present system and bring about conformity to it, *or* it becomes "the practice of freedom," the means by which men and women deal critically and creatively with reality and discover how to participate in the transformation of their world. (Freire, 1996, p. 16)

Although it was not Anay's school experience, an interesting example of Shaull's second purpose of education is evident in rural schooling in another Mexican state. The Zapatista Army of National Liberation was opposed to some of the policies in the North American Free Trade Agreement and other economic and political actions that resulted in conditions they found oppressive to the indigenous residents of southern Mexico. The Zapatistas' proposals for justice had a strong focus on education, along with demands for health, infrastructure, and democracy.

The Zapatistas have formed their own schools—autonomous, with no government funding or regulations. Their curriculum is based in critical pedagogy and inquiry so that the children can learn their cultural history, their native language, and the economic and political forces that affect their way of life. Equitable education for girls is a mandate. Teachers are the servants of the community; they receive no salary and the community members provide for their needs.[2]

After elementary school, Mexicans attend *secundaria*. Although the U.S. junior high and the Mexican *secundaria* cover the same grades—seventh through ninth—they are not equal. Mexican education is subject to that tug that Schaull describes above—preparing students to enter society as it exists to maintain conformity, or providing an education with critical thought and the opportunity for transformation within the individual and the society. In the early 1990s, when *secundaria* became compulsory in Mexico, several types of these schools were formed. One delivers a more traditional curriculum intended for students who will continue their education into high school and perhaps university. The technical *secundaria* provides a curriculum that prepares students to enter jobs that are in the community at the cost of a more open, liberal arts curriculum. I visited one such technical school located directly across the street from a very large maquiladora in Ciudad Juárez. All students went through basic technical education with a year's training in how to work on a maquiladora assembly line. One other type of *secundaria* that I will mention has met with some success:

the *telesecundaria*. In very remote areas, the curriculum is sent electronically in the form of video to a community receiver in a central location. A facilitator manages the equipment, takes roll, and administers exams.

Mexico also provides alternative *secundarias* such as one I visited in the state of Puebla. The school was created to provide career options for young people who live in rural areas. There was no entrance test, and students who had little, if any, literacy skills could still attend. The curriculum included workshops to learn about auto mechanics, a set of classes for sewing (the final project was a complete uniform for the local police), tutoring for primary and secondary education studies, and a workshop in how to make the intricate clay sculpture called *árbol de vida* (tree of life). One of these large, brightly painted sculptures, purchased on one of my trips to Mexico, sits on a shelf in my bedroom. Christian religious figures such as Moses and angels dominate the composition, with, I suppose, a brown-skinned, white-haired God near the top holding the earth in his right arm. Making the clay *árbol de vida* is an ancient tradition in this community, and the school wanted to maintain that tradition.

I interviewed the school's administrator and felt her pride in the school's success in providing open and free education to students who would not have access otherwise as well as in its mission to maintain community traditions. I commend her for the school's contribution to the community, but I wonder about the purpose of one strand of the curriculum. A maquiladora that manufactured athletic clothing for U.S. markets was also located in the area. This factory had a partnership with the school. The factory provided sewing machines to the school, and the students did their internships in the factory. Those who were the best seamstresses (almost all the students were women) moved into jobs in that factory, well trained and ready to meet the high quotas that served the factory's needs. I visited inside the factory and remember the view of scores of young women, almost hidden behind the tall stacks of identical pieces of fabric piled on their sewing machines, each worker joining two pieces of cloth, sewing a seam, and then passing it to her neighbor—over and over and over. The women sew, the factory sells more items, we get cheaper garments. The educational model of this *secundaria* echoed Richard Shaull's words and the early Spanish-run colonial school experiences—schooling designed to conform citizens to the dominant system.

Since Anay was sent out to work instead of attending *secundaria*, she missed the acceptable age window to enter public school at this level. She found an alternative in the *secundaria* curriculum provided by the Mexican adult education program—that self-paced program series of about thirty books covering a variety of subjects that Anay was working through when I met her at the church in Ciudad Juárez.

| FOUR |

Ofelia and the Move to Ciudad Juárez

Anay entered a new phase of her life when she moved to Ciudad Juárez, where she met her husband and began her family. To better understand Anay's history and her move to the border, we will meet Anay's mother and examine her role in bringing Anay north to Ciudad Juárez.

In Spanish, the term for giving birth is *dar a luz* (to give light, or to bring to light). Anay's mother, Ofelia, was the little fourteen-year-old who gave light to Anay while her own world was a fog of ignorance, superstition, and punishment. Ofelia herself is a victim of time, location, and experiences. Her story here is born of Anay's memories and emotions, and once more removed from the actual events, as my interpretations, emotions, and concern for Anay flavor the phrases. I pieced together several years' worth of Anay's comments and short conversations to form an account of these early events. Examining this curious mother-daughter relationship may broaden our views and ways of thinking about family and how we interact in family settings.

Eva and Francisco had twelve sons and two daughters. Ofelia was the last child. Anay knows very little about the first daughter. One evening, we were eating tacos in downtown Huixpan when Anay told me what she knew about her only aunt. "My mother was the baby of the family. Grandmother's third child was the only other daughter. I don't know why, but they gave her away to Grandfather's sister. I only saw her a few times. But

Grandfather's sister, my great aunt, was a prostitute. She had her business just one street over—right over there. That was the street for the prostitutes. They are both dead now. I don't think my aunt was a prostitute, but she helped run the business."

Ofelia grew up while Eva was still drinking heavily. This was a family with few financial resources, and they were steeped in traditions about what daughters should do and how they should contribute to the family. In that community and that time, a man had to show his financial ability to support a wife by sharing resources with the future bride's parents. In their conversations, I heard family members phrase this in terms of "buying the girl"; thus she was his possession. At fourteen, Ofelia was pregnant. There were two men in her life, a teacher and a man friend with whom she lived after Eva and Francisco demanded that she leave their house. Eventually, she ended up with a third man, Don Arturo. Unknown are the circumstances about her separation from her baby, Anay. Perhaps this was her choice, or perhaps she was helpless under the commands of her parents. Eventually, when Anay was a baby, Ofelia and the old man, Don Arturo, moved to be near her parents.

"Grandfather wouldn't let her marry the teacher because he didn't have enough money to buy my mother. I think she just wanted to get out of that house. They treated her like a slave. So she moved in with Don Arturo. He was as old as my grandfather! He already had a family with children, some older than my mother! But his wife left him and took everything, so he didn't have any money. They were very poor when they started living together. For a few years, they lived in a small hut near my grandparents. My mother grew flowers on this land. She had the prettiest garden around.

"One day, though, they had a big argument with my grandparents. I remember that Grandmother threw a lit oil lamp at Don Arturo's feet. Don Arturo had some family who lived in Santa Teresa in [a nearby state]. They owned a store, and Don Arturo thought maybe he could work at that store. So they packed up and got on the train the next day and moved to Santa Teresa.

"My mother wanted to grow her flowers to sell for the Day

of the Dead celebration. But that land didn't serve for anything; it was too close to the ocean. So she went back to Huixpan on the train. She went back to her old house. She loaded that good soil up in bags, and carried it to the new house. I don't know how many trips she made carrying those bags of dirt . . . ouuuu . . . many. But, she did get those flowers to grow in Santa Teresa. She made some money that way."[1]

On our day at the beach, Anay told me another story from the time when she stayed in her mother's home. Lining the beach were a few small restaurants with thatched roofs opening out to the bay. We had arrived early Sunday morning and sat down at a table under the palm-topped shade of the only restaurant that was open. A young woman came out and said, "I'm sorry. All we have to serve now is shrimp soup." The shrimp were the size of cigars and seasoned with chile and cilantro. Quite a breakfast. While we were eating, I learned that Anay had lived with her mother in Santa Teresa during some of the summers of her elementary years. She worked yet another job to help with the family economy. "You know, I used to peel shrimp in a shrimp factory. I would get up at 4:00 A.M. and peel until 10:00 A.M. You bend them back like this and take out the intestines and stuff. I could do it very fast. That was when we had school vacations, and I would go stay with my mother. That was in April and one or two months in the summer. That factory was close to where my mom lived by the ocean by Santa Teresa. I'd walk there. They did pay me, but I had to give it to my mother, and she gave some of it to Grandmother Eva."

One day in 1998 (Anay was back with Grandmother Eva then), a van drove into Santa Teresa. The driver was associated with one of the maquiladoras located in Ciudad Juárez. The van driver visited around the town and told the people that there was good work in the maquiladoras. They could get about ten dollars a day, and with overtime, sometimes up to twelve a day. This included social services provided by the government for basic medical care and a contribution to retirement. His van would take them to the city. The maquiladora would provide a house for them until they could get established.

The offer attracted Ofelia. In planning her budget, no doubt she was unaware of the difference in costs of living in these two communities. For example, fruit, so abundant—an arm's length away in tropical Mexico—is imported and very costly in the desert area around the border. Housing and transportation are also more costly. Nevertheless, she and her twelve-year-old son signed on. The van driver charged the equivalent of $150 to each of them for the trip (this amount was later deducted from Ofelia's first paychecks). Mother and son joined the van full of travelers for the four-day-long drive spanning the length of Mexico. The sixteen van riders paid for all their own food and drink and slept on their own blankets on the ground. When they reached Ciudad Juárez, the van dropped them off at a one-room apartment. They could stay there for one week at no cost. After that, they had to find another place to live, or the factory would deduct rent from their paychecks. Don Arturo and the other two children moved north to join Ofelia a few months later.

At that time, there was a great demand for laborers in these factories. By 2002, Ciudad Juárez hosted about 250 foreign-owned factories as described in the introduction to this book, and the city had the largest maquiladora workforce in all of Mexico. Ofelia signed on with Harnesses of Juárez, a factory so large that it spread over multiple plants. The majority of the laborers in this factory spent their days attaching electric cables to the metal harnesses that organize the electric components in various U.S.-made automobiles.

An economic surge in the late 1990s attracted more and more factories to Ciudad Juárez, and laborers were enticed with incentives like low-interest loans for housing, child care, health care, free birth control (cheaper than paying for maternity leave), and free education. Of course, all of these incentives came with strings attached and were subject to the whims of the company's economic concerns. Some of these employees told me that the birth control pills were always free, the housing loans were only for workers who had been employed there a long time with excellent attendance, and the wait time to get into the clinics could run from three to fifteen hours.

Ofelia's factory provided benefits, one of which was assistance in attaining a certificate for completing elementary, middle, or high school. The factory allowed employees to stay at the facility after hours, and the company would provide a room and a tutor to assist employees enrolled in an open education program for adults, the Instituto Nacional de Educación para Adultos (National Institute for Adult Education), provided by the government. The offer was limited to only a small number of employees, and it could be withdrawn when the labor force exceeded the factory's demand for labor. Often, this incentive was offered only to employees with good attendance records.

This adult education program was basically the same one that Anay was studying when I met her at the church in Ciudad Juárez. The curriculum consisted of a series of books similar to those used in typical U.S. correspondence courses. After reading and successfully passing a test on each of the more than thirty books covering basic subject matter for *secundaria*, a student could get a diploma. The students could continue in a similar process for a high school degree. Fees were charged for each test and for the diploma. This open program for adult education did provide low-cost education that was accessible in almost all parts of the country, but it was not easy to endure the effort alone, plowing through book after book in this independent, self-guided approach to learning. In my previous research, I found that only a very small percentage completed the full course of studies, even with tutoring provided by the factories or other organizations (Hampton, 2004).

The employees who took advantage of the maquiladora assistance for education were faced with an additional problem: transportation. The maquiladoras provided transportation to their employees in a fleet of used buses that traveled from centralized locations in the city to the factory on a schedule that would allow assembly workers to fill all three eight-hour shifts, thus keeping the factory running twenty-four hours per day. These central locations for the maquiladora bus stops were, for most workers, several miles from their homes, so they had a long walk added to the long workday and the long bus rides. There were no alternative bus routes, and no additional transportation was provided for those who were involved in the after-work education program. They were left to rely on the city bus system or to wait several hours for a factory bus that served a later shift.

Ofelia's factory offered a bonus to employees who recruited other employees to sign up to work one of the shifts. Ofelia called her parents and told them that Anay should move to Ciudad Juárez and live with her to help take care of her children. When she turned sixteen, the eligible work age, she could sign on with Harnesses of Juárez and, after hours, do what she had always wanted to do: continue her education. Eva and Francisco would have one less mouth to feed, and Ofelia would get the bonus.

ANAY MOVES TO CIUDAD JUÁREZ

Grandfather Francisco did not want Anay to make that trip alone, so in June 1999, he and Anay took the train to Santa Teresa to catch the maquiladora van.

"That driver charged [the equivalent of $350] for both of us to go to Juárez. It was a fifteen-passenger van, but he loaded sixteen of us on it! And all our stuff. We were packed in there tight! He said that he owned the van, but the maquiladoras hired him to bring these people to work for them. That is his job—to keep making those trips back and forth, back and forth [the round-trip is more than 2,500 miles]. On the very first day of the trip, that van broke down. We all got out and just stayed by the side of the road for many hours while the driver walked to some place where he could get help. So he fixed the van that time and off we go. No, we didn't sleep in a hotel! We just rolled out a blanket and slept on the ground by the van! The second day . . . that van broke down again. It just kept on breaking down. Everybody's food and water was running out. The driver kept calling the maquiladora on his cell phone to say that we were late. Do you know what I heard him say? He told them, 'I have the cargo here, but the delivery will be late.' He didn't even say we were people, just cargo.

"That van kept breaking and breaking, and we stayed out in the open. No baths, nothing! It took us eleven days to get to Juárez! My grandfather and I had eaten all our food. When we stopped at a gas station we could get some water to drink, and we had a little money. So, we bought crackers and chips for a few days. Then our money ran out. I had a little gold ring that my cousin gave me. At one gas station, we took that ring to a lady and her husband sitting in their car and asked if they would buy it. They bought it for [the equivalent of $5]. We used that to buy food for the last days. When we got to Juárez, we hadn't eaten or had anything to drink for more than twenty-four hours! When we got there my mother and grandmother were so scared. They had not heard anything about us."

Anay moved in with Ofelia. By now, Ofelia had three children. Anay helped care for them in the daytime and worked in a convenience store in the evenings, biding her time until she turned sixteen, the official age to work in a maquiladora. She worked long hours at the convenience store, sometimes twenty-four-hour shifts, and received the equivalent of about fifty dollars per week.

When she turned sixteen, she entered the workforce at Harnesses of Juárez. Her first position there was on the assembly line, but soon she advanced to training new assembly line workers. One day she became ill and asked her supervisor if she could visit the factory's clinic. The supervisor refused to let her. Anay pushed the issue and asked again, claiming her right, and the supervisor fired her after nine months at the factory. She went back to working at the convenience store.

THE STEPFATHER, DON ARTURO

The following account describes Anay's subjection to abuse from her stepfather while living with him and Ofelia in Ciudad Juárez, and also when she was very young. I cannot report, or even sense, the extent of Anay's emotional scars over this abuse. To me, she is a strong woman with an optimistic attitude, but she melted emotionally as she described one of these events to me.

Don Arturo, the old man with whom her mother had lived since Anay was a baby, sexually abused Anay over the years when she was very young. Of course, the real "truth" about sexual abuse for very young girls is illusive. Children's memories develop along with their bodies and their emotions. These developments get stifled in an abusive situation. Abuse in the vital context of familial love may confuse a little child seeking closeness and family.

Anay only offered a little information about this abuse, but it was verified by a medical doctor. Shortly after the birth of her fourth child, she became very ill and was hospitalized. I visited her in the clinic in Ciudad Juárez and met her doctor. I overheard him describe Anay's condition to Enrique. "She was a mess—from the four children and the early abuse. The wall between the colon and the cervix was almost gone, and cancerous tumors formed from the traumas in her uterus. I think I got all of the tumors when I took out her uterus, and I reconstructed the wall for the colon. She's tough; this just might work."

She couldn't afford the clinic for more than a few days, so he gave her strong medications to keep her resting in bed and to combat the cancer. Enrique managed to care for four children and a sick wife for many weeks. I still admire that doctor. He told me that he had a practice in El Paso and also worked in Ciudad Juárez. He charged a small fraction of what he would have charged in El Paso. Anay regained her strength in a few months, although the cancer reappeared, as I discuss later.

Anay lived with Francisco and Eva when she was little, but on some weekends, as described earlier, she would visit her mother. She told me that from her earliest memory, she sees Don Arturo in the bed with her. She remembers holding a baby bottle and seeing his big legs over her. As a little girl, he told her it was a game. She thought this was the way that fathers played with their daughters. Later on, she was able to tell him that she did not like it.

In homes so small and so public, individual rooms and individual beds seldom exist. Anay told me, "When I was at my mother's house, I slept with my brothers and sisters. Héctor [her brother] would sleep across my feet to protect me. Neither of us slept much." Maybe a loud protest from his son would deter the old man.

When her mother and Don Arturo moved north to Juárez, Anay was safe—until she moved in with them as a teenager. Then he tried it again. One day she was in the bathroom taking a shower. She called it a "shower," but with no running water, it was really a sponge bath. There was only a sheet over the door. He came in, stood behind her, and grabbed her breasts. She was able to slip out of his grasp and she fled out the front door screaming. There was no opportunity to grab a covering, so she was running naked in the street. She ran to a neighbor's house crying at the door, but no one was home. She tried two more houses before someone was home to let her in and wrap her in a blanket.

When Anay told me the story of the attempted rape from Don Arturo, her anger came out in the account, but she spoke clearly and directly. With this last sentence, she began to cry uncontrollably for most of an hour. Through the hiccuping sobs, she finally managed to say, "My mother saw it all and told me it was my fault!" Our language is lacking an expletive strong enough to express my anger and rage at the injustice. Which is worse? To be raped by your "father" or to be accused by your mother? Together they can constitute a fatal blow to familial love.

We sat in my car while sweet Enrique played with all the kids at Peter Piper Pizza in Ciudad Juárez. I just held her and let her cry and sob for that hour. That was the point when she started calling me Mommy. "You are the only person who hugs me and calls me precious. You are the only one who has ever taken us to a restaurant." When Enrique talks to Anay about me, he calls me "your mother." When he talks about her biological mother, he uses her first name, Ofelia. When Anay gets particularly blue, Enrique tells her to call me or come see me. He always hugs me and encourages our visits. I guess it gives her strength to climb up one more step or hang onto the ladder a little tighter. All I can do is listen and comfort. I'm glad I can help, but I do know it is a projection of a love that she so desperately missed.

I was able to remain in close contact with Anay, Enrique, and their growing family during the early years of the first decade of this century. They welcomed my visits any time, and from time to time, Anay would call me when they were able to cross into El Paso. We took every opportunity to see each other. These were the years when she was building a home, a family, and a career.

ENRIQUE, THE CHILDREN, AND THE MISSION

When she moved to Ciudad Juárez, Anay did not know anyone outside of her mother's family. A neighbor invited her to go to a Christian church as her guest. She was fifteen, and she attended the class for teenagers. Her teacher was Enrique, a handsome man about ten years her senior. His dark skin and high cheekbones bespeak his Indian heritage, and he proudly claims his Apache forefathers. He had just finished a training program in Torreón, Mexico, to get a certificate to be a preacher for the *Iglesia de Cristo* (Church of Christ) and was serving as the youth minister for this church. For two years, that was the extent of their relationship. When she was seventeen, she became very ill and was in the hospital. She had no one to care for her or help with the bills, so she called on her youth minister. Their love grew from that experience, and they married a few months later.

"Enrique is a very patient man! I couldn't have sex with him right after we were married. When he tried to touch my breasts, I jumped away, thinking about when the old man would grab my breasts and squeeze so hard. Enrique was so patient and so slow and so tender. He just waited and took it so slowly. But also I was bleeding all the time. The doctor said it was because of the abuse. So I never knew when I could get pregnant. We tried everything. Because of all the sores, a condom felt like glass cutting me. I tried the pill and threw it up. I tried the apparatus, but it came out with all the blood. The doctor told me, 'Don't worry. You won't get pregnant. Just in case, here are the days when you are not ovulating.' So we tried very slow and difficult sex on those days. We only had sex a very few times. But, with most of them, I got pregnant!

"I got pregnant with Eva a few months after we were married. Enrique was so happy. One of his brothers could not have children, and he didn't think he could ever have children, and he was thirty years old. When she was born, he slept every night with her like this [she indicated in the crook of his arm]. She was a good baby, and I was happy for Enrique. But no more. I wanted to finish my education before I had any more children. This was my goal forever!"

On one of my early visits with Anay while they were living at the church, we went for a walk with baby Eva on that same dusty alley-like road in front of the church building. We talked a while about what she was reading in her school books. She was very close to finishing the *secundaria* program. Suddenly she burst into tears and said, "I'm pregnant again. Now all my plans are reversed!"

About the time that the second baby, Juliet, was born, Enrique got a job working as a missionary for the Church of Christ. A congregation in El Paso, Texas, paid him about three hundred dollars per month to minister to a high-poverty community in southern Ciudad Juárez. Most of the residents in this community are like Anay in that they have come from other parts of Mexico to work in the maquiladoras. There are no paved roads in this community, only sandy, rocky trails. Their houses initially are made of scrap materials, mostly packing pallets set on end with tar paper over them. Old tires hold the roof on the shed. As families gather a few resources, they start to purchase concrete block and build, room by room, their block houses.

Part of Enrique's job was to teach Bible classes to the Spanish-speaking church members in El Paso, so he and Anay crossed into El Paso several times a week. Anay met a woman from the El Paso church who needed someone to help her clean and cook. The woman allowed Anay and little Eva to live with her in El Paso for a few months before the new baby was born. So baby Juliet was born in an El Paso hospital and thus has dual citizenship in Mexico and the United States. I visited Anay in the hospital the day after Juliet was born. Anay seemed to be quite in love with the new baby, and I thought she was beautiful. Enrique quit his job at the maquiladora for a while and was able to be home a little more to help out with the children. Anay was able to finish her *secundaria* curriculum in a few months.

With his new missionary job, Anay and Enrique were able to build a home in the same high-poverty community where Enrique was doing his mission work. Church members from the United States came to visit the new mission and the emerging community. They provided some money to Enrique and Anay to build a small structure of concrete block, with the understanding that the new mission church would meet in the Carrillos' living room. Some of these church members helped Enrique build the first two rooms of the home. Enrique kept adding to the house, so that after five years, there were three bedrooms, a living room and kitchen, and a bathroom. Enrique dug a septic tank and put in a flushing toilet (still no running water, however). Donated furnishings and handed-down toys and clothes soon filled the house. The water-damaged wedding photo and Enrique's preaching diploma hung in the living room. They did not have enough money to paint the outside of the house, but Enrique found a can of red paint and proudly painted on the outside of the gray blocks "Iglesia de Cristo." They lived in this house for most of the years of our close friendship.

The landowners charged about seven thousand dollars for this tiny parcel of desert land with no infrastructure and no zoning regulations. A scrap metal shop full of wrecked cars was built between the neighborhood and the street, only yards from Anay's home.

The residents of this and other emergent neighborhoods on the outskirts of the city had no utility infrastructure, so they pirated the electricity from the closest main utility line. This was Enrique and Anay's source of electricity also. I remember cringing as my car drove over scores of electric cables running from the main line, drooping down and draping over the sandy road, then snaking through the windows of the various houses. From the window, the cable was attached to extension cords to run electrical appliances. The city government soon came in and provided official electricity. Basically, it is the same system, but the coupling to the main line is safer, and the residents are now charged for the service. As the price of copper increased, sometimes someone cut this line from the main cable to the houses to sell the wire. Enrique has had to replace their copper electric wires twice.

On Thursday mornings (hopefully) the water truck came by, and the driver blasted the *ooo-gahh* horn to announce his arrival. If someone was at home when he arrived, he or she would meet him outside, pay the driver the four dollars, and the driver would fill their barrels and tanks with water from the truck. One of the most important resources in this desert land is water, or *agua*, in Spanish. Although some parts of Ciudad Juárez are actually on the banks of the Rio Grande, that stretch of the river is U.S. property, and the Mexicans are not permitted to touch the river. The Mexicans' name for the river is Río Bravo, Brave River; but this brave border line between El Paso and Ciudad Juárez is a dry bed most of the year—denied its own water but for the few summer months when it serves as a channel to deliver water allocations to irrigate the desert's agricultural industry. Before the attacks on the twin towers in New York on September 11, 2001, in the summer months, we would see Mexicans playing along the river bank or washing their cars with the river water. Now, Border Patrol officers are stationed all along the river, peering from the U.S. side into every sandy inch of the Mexican shore, forbidding access.

The communities on the outskirts of Ciudad Juárez are all built in the sandhills. Whatever desert shrubs did grow on the hills have long been stripped and burned as firewood. Old plastic bags wave in the wind from their snags on weeds and thorn bushes. No pools, no streams, no running water . . . just sand and trash. The residents all depended on the water trucks to deliver water. But this water is not approved for drinking, so they have to purchase more expensive water in plastic containers for drinking and cooking, or boil the water that the truck delivers. Anay carried water from a barrel in front of the house to a little propane burner to heat water for washing everything—dishes, clothes, and the babies. Around Christmas of 2005, the water delivery truck did not come for two weeks. Enrique just laughed as he told me, "We were sure stinky that week."

In the summer of 2007, we had another set of rainstorms, with five to seven inches falling in some areas within a few hours. This caused flooding in many parts of El Paso and Ciudad Juárez. I knew the flooding was worse in Ciudad Juárez, but I could not contact Anay. I had to sit and wait. After several days, she was able to find a phone to call me and said that their entire neighborhood was underwater. Their house sits a little higher than the others, so only about one inch of water got into her house. However, it was a virtual lake for about a mile around them. For days they could not get out. No cars could get through, and the main street to their neighborhood was closed. Finally, Enrique walked through the water, hip-high at times, for about a mile to a convenience store to buy water and a little food. By the time she called me, the floodwater was starting to go down, and she assured me they were fine—a little hungry and a little dirty. Short of renting a helicopter, there was nothing I could do to help her.

CROSS-BORDER SUPPORT

Other Church of Christ groups in Texas and Oklahoma have worked with the El Paso church to conduct mission projects in Ciudad Juárez. Usually they ran these out of Anay and Enrique's home. Sometimes they brought in doctors and nurses, and the neighbors came for medical assistance. Sometimes they hosted Vacation Bible School, where young people from the center of the United States get to interact with Mexican children.

These friends helped Enrique and Anay's family and after a few years built their small church building just down the . . . well, it's not a street, it's a dusty path that cars can barely drive on. Near the church they added a little playground, which was destroyed in a few months by the bigger kids in the community. Anay expressed to me that she was happy that they built the church building. She said that hosting the church service in her home three times a week brought some problems with missing items and the need to stretch her family's scarce supplies of water and food to the large groups.

Many interactions with the U.S. church groups, such as those mentioned above, do provide support, but that gets complicated. The neighbors in the community consider the Carrillos the "rich" family. Because of their U.S. church friends, they do have much more than most of their neighbors. Many of the homes are not as big as the Carrillo home. The church groups often bring bags of used clothing and toys to give to the church members. This places Anay in the difficult position of distributing the items fairly. When she does distribute them, only some of the neighbors get clothes, and Anay gets complaints. Those left out of the distribution often claim that she is playing favorites or keeping items for herself.

One of the church families from the United States sold a used van to Anay and Enrique. This was big enough to hold all their children, but soon it was also in high demand by the community. Very few of their neighbors had cars, and Enrique was often called upon to take someone to an important doctor's appointment or job interview. Gasoline costs were high. Also, the neighbors dropped in on the preacher's family frequently, usually around mealtime. Enrique and Anay could not manage to provide all of this assistance to the people in the neighborhood on his small salary, so he set limits. They fenced their house and locked the fence. When the van wore out, they sold it as scrap for less than a hundred dollars, and several of us pitched in to get them a small, economical car that would hold only their family.

Church groups from the United States continued to direct missionary activities out of Anay and Enrique's home—two or three per year. They provided valuable assistance and perhaps should have felt satisfied when they returned to their comfortable homes, knowing that their efforts helped those in poverty. However, for Anay and Enrique, meeting this flood of basic needs on a continual basis was nearly impossible to sustain as fellow members of their low-income community. With minimal resources, this work amounted to triage. Enrique likes to preach and teach Bible classes, and he is generous and giving. People streamed in and out of their house, but he and Anay had to draw a line and deny many requests for services. As the new babies came along, Elaine in 2004 and son Enrique (Kiké) in 2005, the family became a mission of its own.

In 2004, when they received the van from El Paso church friends, Enrique saw an opportunity to take his family home to southern Mexico so that Eva and Francisco could see their grandchildren (three at this time). The van was old and big, which translated to expensive gas bills. The price of gas for those hundreds of miles was far outside their financial means. Ofelia said she would pay the gas if she could go with them, so they all loaded up and made the trip to Huixpan. After a few days in Huixpan, without warning, Ofelia got on the bus and returned to Ciudad Juárez, taking the gas money for the return trip with her. They were stuck. Uncle Lalo loaned Enrique money for a bus ride back to Ciudad Juárez so he could find money to bring the family home.

I asked Enrique what he did to get that money. He held up his ring hand and pointed to the empty third finger. Hocking his wedding ring wasn't enough, however, so he sold some items in the house, borrowed a little here and there, and worked double shifts at a maquiladora until he had the few hundred dollars to pay for his bus trips and the gasoline for the van. Two friends said they would pay a little if they could ride to the border with them. Altogether, it was a month before the family and the van arrived back home.

A MOTHER'S ROLE

For better or worse, Ofelia brought Anay to Ciudad Juárez. Ofelia still lives with Don Arturo, who was 86 years old as we finished this book. Ofelia's last child was born the same time as Anay's third baby, when Don Arturo was 83. Anay told me, "Do the math! I don't understand it. I don't know if any of the children are his . . . maybe Héctor. But he is so cruel to all of them and yells, 'Get out of here. You are nothing to me. You son of a bitch.' I keep asking my little sister if he is hurting her. She says, 'No. It's okay.' So, I hope it is. Little Héctor wants to go to school, but they don't help him. Enrique and I help him some. I don't know why they are together. I hate to go see them, so we don't go over there much. She comes to see me when she needs something. But never to see the children, or birthdays. And she never helps us with money."

Although Ofelia's role as mother to Anay is not exemplary, Enrique did provide some insight that helps understand her. "Because Anay was raised by Eva and Francisco, Ofelia thinks of her as a sister, not a daughter. She acts more like Anay is her sister."

So, here is Anay, a young, intelligent woman with four unplanned children born in rapid succession and with a history of extreme familial abuse. Would she repeat the violence? Although I did not live with Anay, I did visit often enough to observe the family dynamic. Once I asked her if her past affected the way she deals with the children. She told me about her struggle to avoid violence when disciplining the children.

"It is hard having the kids so close together. And sometimes I don't feel too good and I am so tired. One time, Juliet was crying and crying, and Eva had made a big mess, and I just started hitting them. Enrique grabbed my hand and said, 'Don't ever beat my children!' And I look at how you play with the girls and treat them gently, and Enrique shows me how to love. I don't beat them now, but sometimes I get so frustrated. I know I have to break that custom that I learned from my grandmother."

The night before Anay and I took off for our trip to her family home, I spent the night with them in their house in the maquiladora community so we could catch an early flight out of the airport in Ciudad Juárez. I arrived about 7:30 that night. Enrique left at 8:30 to pick Anay up from her school. The kids and I played and read books. It was close to 10:00 when Enrique and Anay returned. They had been to the grocery store. Anay's brother, Héctor, and his wife, Suzi, had agreed to stay in the house and help Enrique watch the kids while we were gone. The children had a bowl of cereal and got ready to go to bed. Eva kissed us all good night and went to bed with Héctor and Suzi. We all slept in the three small consecutive rooms—open to each other. Juliet and I shared a small bed. I huddled in a corner to change into my gown and noticed Juliet, Elaine, and little Kiké piled up on their mother and daddy's bed with Anay in the middle of the pile. Anay held the book, little Enrique was on one side, Elaine on the other side, and Juliet was lying across Anay's stomach—all intent as Anay read three books. That is their nightly ritual. After the stories, Juliet joined me, and we settled down for a restless, hot night.

"Sometimes I read books to them, but sometimes I tell them stories about Ana Rana [little frog]. That is what Grandfather used to call me. He would sing to me in the morning, 'Ana Rana, time to get out of bed. Ana Rana, time to go to school. Ana Rana, time to sell the fish.' I love my Grandfather. I have no memories of him ever hitting me or yelling at me. He was always quiet and gentle.

"So, I tell the girls the story of little Ana Rana and how she had to sell fruit in the streets. I don't tell them that it was me. They think it is a little frog. I tell them about how she got in trouble if she did not sell all the fruit, and how she wanted to go to school, and how she was the smartest frog in the class. And they laugh when I tell about the time that Ana Rana and her grandmother were chased by bees. They ran as fast as they could, and finally the bees went somewhere else. But Grandmother was looking behind her when she ran into a cow and flipped over the cow. They laugh and laugh at that story.

"Did you know that Enrique has a tattoo? Most people would not think that. Not for a preacher. It is right on his upper thigh. It used to be the name of his old girlfriend. But he had a little frog tattooed over that. He calls the frog Ana Rana."

INTERPRETIVE CONTEXT: DOMESTIC ABUSE

During her childhood, Anay's home and heart was with Grandmother Eva, who obviously loved her. Unfortunately, with Eva's own background and alcohol's encouragement, Anay was abused physically and emotionally, and she was denied the chance to continue schooling. Yet, Anay spoke lovingly about her grandmother and named her first child Eva. Grandmother Eva's home was safe compared to Ofelia's house, where she was sexually abused by Don Arturo.

Humans abuse each other. Abusers can be found in every social, economic, and racial category. The drunken grandmother. The ostracized and rejected man who lives with your mother. The parent whose life is so driven by self-satisfaction that the child is pushed aside and ignored. The neighbor's brother whose body is dominated by raging hormones. The young soldier, upstanding and honest before battle, now uncontrollably aroused by the testosterone-generating thrill of the hunt, the kill, and the domination. The frustrated and frazzled mother of demanding young children. The teacher who dominates with cruelty out of fear of losing control and power. The sociopath. The pedophile priest. The power-drunk leader. The power-hungry victims of their own childhood abuse. Many of us have abused, and many of us have been abused.

The victims are the vulnerable—most often children and women. The abuse never leaves you. It scars your soul. It stains your memory. It redirects your future. It demands. If you confront it and channel it into an artistic expression or an energetic endeavor, you can live with it. If you try to ignore it, it will creep out of you in monstrous expressions of regenerated abuse.

An Amnesty International 2004 report explains how pov-

erty and marginalization are causal factors in this violence. Political and social situations often leave women on these margins
of society, and that was Anay's position—neither a daughter of
her grandmother nor a daughter of her mother. She was subject to the abuse because she was young, vulnerable, and on the
margin of the family in both of her home settings.

Our tacit knowledge tells us that this kind of violence is
rampant across the globe, and that ignorance increases it, domination feeds it, and high-stress social situations spawn it. In
some societies, people have been socialized to accept it.

> Violence against women is not confined to any particular po-
> litical or economic system, but is prevalent in every society in
> the world and cuts across boundaries of wealth, race and cul-
> ture. The power structures within society which perpetuate
> violence against women are deep-rooted and intransigent. The
> experience or threat of violence inhibits women everywhere
> from fully exercising and enjoying their human rights. (Am-
> nesty International, 2004, p. 2)

How does a social scientist count abuse? How can it be cat-
egorized? Abuse stays hidden, underreported, and ill-defined.
That which is reported may be shrouded in a child's developing
memory and emotion or a woman's fear and helplessness. Amnesty International's data on child welfare show that countries
across the globe, including the United States and Latin American countries, have high incidences of child abuse, and the
abuse rates seem to be growing, with figures of domestic violence as high as 50 percent in many parts of the world.

The Aztecs and Mayas had common practices that we would
consider abuse, such as deforming babies' skulls and crossing
their eyes as a sign of beauty, along with violent initiation rites
or cruel punishment for wayward adolescents. Then, with the
Spanish conquest and colonization, raping indigenous women
was often considered a right of the conquering warrior and a de-
sired practice that could lead to the dilution of the native blood
lines to further the goals of the Spanish conquest. Octavio Paz

(1961) in *The Labyrinth of Solitude* posits that much of Mexican thought and action stems from the violence against women that resulted in the birth of the mestizo race.

In some societies in various parts of the world, religious and social practices allow victims to be blamed for the humiliations they endure in their innocence. The children resulting from rapes are often unwanted, abused, and abandoned (Estrada, 2001). The women who suffer the abuse and the children born from it are stigmatized and punished.

When Cortés conquered Mexico City, he seized an intelligent young Aztec woman, Malinztin Tenépal, to serve as his interpreter and concubine. That relationship is not clearly understood, but she accompanied him on most of his missions. History and time changed her name to La Malinche. She had been an Aztec princess, and after the death of her father she was sold into Mayan slavery. She met Cortés when she was fourteen and mastered Spanish in a very short time. She converted to Christianity and became his translator. Octavio Paz paints her as the traitor to Mexican indigenous people by selling them out to the Spaniards. Thus, she becomes the metaphor for the rape of indigenous women and the blame cast upon them. Because of this, Mexican women may be socialized to bear their suffering in silence so they will not be considered a La Malinche–type traitor. According to Flores-Ortiz (1999), this is one reason Mexican women hide domestic abuse: so they will not "betray" the family.

Adelaida Del Castillo (1977) paints La Malinche differently, positing that perhaps her actions stemmed from her Christian conversion. Her strong conviction regarding the sanctity of the Catholic Church, according to Del Castillo, informed her feeling of justification in assisting in the conquest of the native Mexican cultures.

Anthropologist Christine Eber (2000) writes about familial abuse and the use and abuse of alcohol in Mayan communities in Chiapas in her book *Women and Alcohol in a Highland Maya Town*. The dense ethnographic study chronicles many of the complex social interactions that underlie the familial abuses, too complex to summarize succinctly. The abuses are historical, somewhat accepted, and engrained in many segments of the society. Eber and Kovic's more recent (2003) work is a compilation of research showing how women of Chiapas are organizing through social and religious communities to improve women's rights, reduce violence, and reduce the abuse of alcohol. Grandmother Eva, though not from a Mayan community, grew up in a similar culture where she was surrounded by and was a victim of violence.

Laura McClusky's (2001) ethnography examining domestic violence in a Mayan community in Belize, helps us understand some of the tangled cultural and gender complexities that preserve the violence. "It is difficult to keep people front and center: to provide a means for readers to develop emotional understanding, to rehumanize studies of domestic violence, and at the same time to state clear and simple facts and to develop a clear theoretical model for understanding domestic violence cross-culturally" (p. 269). I further explore this violence against women, in the context of maquiladoras, in chapter 6.

Perhaps the historic influences mentioned here do, indeed, prompt some of the ongoing abuse. History and social contexts inform our understanding of inhumane acts. They do not, however, justify the abuses.

FIVE

School in Ciudad Juárez

Anay never let go of her passion to achieve a full education and attend a university. Her successful experiences in elementary school in rural Mexico motivated her, fueling her confidence and determination. Her path to achieving an undergraduate education serves as a window through which we can peer into unique approaches to schooling in Mexican border communities.

TWO TIMES THROUGH *SECUNDARIA*

Ofelia's actions brought Anay to a location where she could continue her education, but she had to struggle up a hill of limited resources and personal delays. The maquiladora where Ofelia worked, Harnesses of Juárez, hired Anay just as she turned sixteen. Anay was delighted because it meant she could go to school. However, "go to school" in the maquiladora environment does not have the same meaning as it does in places with well-funded public education.

In the United States, pre-college schools are free and readily available, by law, for all citizens. Although there are discrepancies in the quality and resources of the schools across different parts of the nation, there are, in general, sufficient public school programs to meet the needs of the population. Public funds provide transportation for any student outside of walking distance, free meals to students who meet certain low-income requirements, and mandatory modified education for students with special needs. I will, of course, add the disclaimer that U.S. schools are far from perfect, as dropout rates are high, unsuccessful curriculum models are often in place, many students and teachers feel threatened and marginalized, and the window for free public education is usually closed by age twenty. However, free and open access to the schooling experience is institutionalized in the United States.

In Mexico, school is free through grade nine; however, as discussed in previous chapters, access to the free education is not always easy, as limited funding for transportation and hidden fees such as uniforms and testing restrict many students from participating. The elementary program is much more successful in Mexico. Most children do have access to an elementary school program, although overcrowding in the cities and long distances in the rural areas negatively affect access. Also, additional resources such as special education support and free meals are neither institutionalized nor common. *Secundaria* and high schools may be funded partially or fully by the state or federal government, but many schools at this level are privately funded by religious or business enterprises. Even with the private and for-profit schools, there are not enough of these secondary schools to serve all of the population. My research found that for communities near the northern border of Mexico, even if everyone had sufficient funds to attend, still only half of the children could find a space in a secondary school (Hampton, 2004).

Attending a regular *secundaria* in Ciudad Juárez was out of the question for Anay. But with this government-sponsored program that the maquiladora hosted—a canned curriculum of independent study with a facilitator/administrator—Anay could "attend school." The curriculum was composed of reading many books and taking a test on each one, a vastly different school experience than those offered by junior high schools or middle schools in the United States. Anay described this school:

"The school was really a room in the maquiladora—a small room, oh, about fifty people could barely fit in there. Señora Emma was the organizer. She wasn't the teacher. Her job was to arrange for someone [a student] to get enrolled in the school, and hire the tutors, and get the students ready for graduation when they finish—all the paperwork and all. I was taking the *secundaria*. There are thirty-two books for this course. I had to read every book and pass a test. I had to buy the book for [the equivalent of about five dollars] and pay [the equivalent of about three dollars] for every test. We were all on different books, so nobody was really teaching us. We just sat in the class and read the books and did the activities. Yvonne was our teacher, but, really, she would just walk up and down the rows and help us when we asked for help . . . yes, more like a tutor. We would stay there for two hours after work for three days each week.

"Did I tell you how I got into that school? There were just fifty spaces, and almost every one of the five hundred or a thousand workers wanted to go to that school. So we had to put our names on a list. I was about number 201. But my mother got into the school a few weeks before I started working there. She didn't like it very much and wanted to quit. Señora Emma knew me because every day I would go to her and say, 'When can I enter the school? When can I enter the school?' Like a little fly, I was very pesky. So when I told her that my mother wanted to quit, she let me go in place of my mother because we had the same last name. Most people thought I was her sister because I used my grandfather's last name like she did—Palomeque."

In 2000, the U.S. economy slipped, and the maquiladora executives began to lay off workers and suspend factory operations. In a few short weeks, many of these factories closed completely. The Harnesses of Juárez plant where Anay worked shut down during that period. All records of her education were lost with that closure. Nevertheless, she did not give up.

"So, I finished all the books pretty fast—like seven months. And I passed the tests. Then, I quit the maquiladora, and they lost all my paperwork when they closed down. I think they did that on purpose. So, I found a Catholic church that was giving the *secundaria* school program. They said I could do the books on my own and take a general test to see if I really had learned that program. I had to work for that test, but I passed it just fine. But they made me pay for all the books again before they would give my papers. Later on, I found that the government gives those books out free! Free! And I had to pay for them twice!"

Anay finally had her papers to show that she had finished the *secundaria*. Then she had another uphill struggle to find access to high school.

BEAUTY SCHOOL AND ANOTHER BABY

In 2002, Anay had finished *secundaria* but did not think it was possible to attend high school with two young children. She and Enrique discussed options. When I visited, we discussed more options. Finally she had a plan. She told me about an opportunity to go to cosmetology school, the Glamour Institute of Ciudad Juárez. She had heard about a government program to help residents start small businesses, so she and Enrique thought that with this degree, they could start a business to augment the small salary he received from the church in El Paso. She would attend school for three hours a day. Enrique would watch Eva and Juliet during that time. It would take about two years to get her degree. I contributed some funds to this effort, and Anay went to school. The program covered hair treatments, nail treatments, skin waxing, and massage. Near the end of the two years, Enrique built some furniture for the beauty salon they planned to open. He made two reception desks that I thought were very well constructed and attractive, with green, marble-looking laminate on the top.

She graduated in 2004, and I was able to attend the graduation ceremony. Ceremonies and celebrations such as this are well attended in Mexico. The school charged a graduation fee, and each attendee had to pay to attend the event. The school had rented a hall, and families sat at tables around a stage. A light dinner was provided. One of Mexico's favorite entertainers is a singer named Juan Gabriel. (Coincidentally, the major street that goes to Anay and Enrique's home is named *Eje Juan Gabriel*.) At the ceremony an impersonator portrayed Juan Gabriel in a very comic and entertaining style. When the show ended, the graduates went forward as their names were called to receive their diplomas.

When she graduated, Anay was pregnant with her third child, so they would have to postpone opening a shop for a few months. She did find work in an existing beauty shop. "I worked for this lady for five hours a day and she paid me only twenty-four pesos per week [about two dollars in U.S. money]. But I stayed there at that ridiculous salary because I needed to have the experience." The reception desks that Enrique had made were turned into storage cabinets in the house.

The third baby girl was born and Anay was very busy taking care of three small children. About a year later, she found herself pregnant again. This pregnancy was more difficult than the others, and she was ill for many months after the birth of baby Kiké, as described previously. The beauty shop idea was lost, along with our investment, or so we thought. A few years later, this training would become very valuable.

THE HIGH SCHOOL, VALLE ALTA

Anay was still determined to get her high school education. As soon as she had delivered her last baby and had her health back, she would attend high school. She searched all through the city for some high school that would accommodate her and the complications her large family brought to her pursuit. Her chances of finding a secondary school that would take her, that she could afford, and that would fit the busy schedule of a mother of four, were slim. In a city such as Ciudad Juárez with a need for a large factory workforce, a higher level of education is not a high priority for government resources. The powerful factory owners agreed to locate there because the city promised to provide large numbers of citizens with minimal education to serve as a reliable source of cheap labor.

In addition, students have to pay to attend high school, and these costs are outside the financial means for many citizens. Because public education at the high school level is not compulsory, there are few public high school facilities, and those charge for their programs. Mexicans with more financial resources send their children to private high schools. Most of these private schools are Catholic. The federal government provides a general core curriculum, and anyone can open a school for profit upon agreement to teach the approved government curriculum. Unfortunately, these enterprises are not always honest. Enrique took classes part time for two years from a private organization claiming to provide a *secundaria* diploma. He paid the equivalent of about four hundred dollars and later discovered that the program was not certified; his work did not count toward a diploma.

One woman, Carla Luján, started three high schools in Ciudad Juárez (pseudonyms are used for the school, staff, and students). All three operated in low-income communities where many residents were maquiladora workers. Carla Luján's sons, Adán and Fernie, with business degrees from the University of Texas at El Paso, managed the schools. In one of these schools, the morning session was for teenagers, and an evening session was offered to older maquiladora employees. The school had a partnership with one of the maquiladoras, Davol Surgical Innovations. Davol management was interested in rewarding good workers with seniority by paying for their high school education. This would prepare them to interact with English-speaking clients or to take on more responsibility in the financial or technical areas of the factory. The majority of students in the evening session at the high school were employees in the Davol maquiladora.

I have explored these kinds of relationships between factories and local schools in my ongoing research and have found the Davol factory's generous level of educational support to be outside of the norm; most maquiladoras provide minimal, if any, support to further education for general employees who work on assembly line. Anay searched throughout the city for high school options that would work for her and eventually found Ms. Luján's school. She applied and was accepted into the evening program of the Valle Alta high school. The fees were reasonable, and some contributions from friends in the United States helped fund her studies.

This school received no government support, but Anay said that she thought they had funding from an international grant. Each student paid the equivalent of about fifty dollars per month plus an extra government certification fee of more than one hundred dollars per year. This allowed the students to receive their government-approved diploma upon graduation with no extra fees. On top of this, there was a final exam fee of about thirty dollars for each class.

Finally, Anay could see her goal almost in hand. She would be able to finish high school and graduate. The school provided a fast-track, year-round curriculum so that the students could finish in two years. The last baby was here, and it looked like she and Enrique could handle this large family. She could study in the daytime while juggling the kids and go to school in the evening when Enrique could watch the children. She was getting her strength back after the birth of the last baby. The school director was very pleased with Anay's admission test scores and her academic strength and had an encouraging conversation with her about options that might be open to her after she graduated. She was elated.

CANCER

One night at school, Anay fainted and fell down a few stairs. This left her temporarily paralyzed in one leg. She went to a clinic the next morning. The medical staff there sent her to a gynecological specialist because of her ongoing bleeding and uterine pain. As soon as I could, I went to the house to see her. That was a few days after she met with the specialist. She and I sat on the bed. The little girls hung close to us—Elaine in my lap, Juliet on Anay's knees, and Eva refusing to leave Anay's side. Anay cried and cried. Finally, she drew a big breath and blew her nose with her fingers, the way I watched my dad do. Tissue and toilet paper are necessities on my side of the border; they are luxuries in Anay's world. That seemed to clear her head enough to tell me the story.

"The cancer came back. It is in the uterus and spreading. There is no wall between my cervix and my anus; I think from the old man's abuse. The doctor has to do an emergency operation to repair my cervix and see how far it has spread. And, look at this MRI of my brain. See, here is my X-ray. There is a swollen area right there, and that is why my leg would not work."

We all hugged and rocked together for a long time until she cried it out again. Then, grabbing onto some sense of hope in the future, she stood up, knocking the kids off of her legs. She looked straight ahead into the wall with her jaw set and said, "Enrique said we will think positive. I'll be okay." With that, she stopped crying and pulled deeply from her well of determination, resistance, and positive power. I had just witnessed a surge of woman strength that allowed her essence to rise again—some high-powered propellant for her hope.

Six months later, after the successful operation by the same good doctor, another cocktail of cancer-attacking chemicals, painkillers, anti-depressants, and vitamins, and her husband's support and love, she was functioning like her old self. I visited a few times during this recuperation. For the first weeks, the medication kept her bedfast and not very cognizant. She said that Enrique once found her trying to cook a towel for dinner, so he wouldn't let her get up very much. She had some horrible days and went through many weeks of depression. As she was able to reduce the drugs, she took on a few tasks and could entertain the children in sedentary activities. I fussed at her one Sunday when I caught her cooking lunch for the people at her church, but she assured me that she was on only a few drugs and was feeling very well.

Anay told the director of Valle Alta about the operation and the long recovery. Ms. Luján said that Anay could stay enrolled in the school. When she felt like it, she could take one class at a time. She could progress at her own pace as she gained her strength back. When she was well, Anay attended classes Monday through Friday from 4:30 to 8:30 P.M. The school consisted of eight classes each semester, and there were three semesters in the year-round schedule to accomplish the two-year curriculum. Some of her teachers let her finish a semester by sending lessons by e-mail. Often, she would do assignments, and Enrique would take them to school for her and pick up other assignments. Anay doubled up on some classes, tested out of a few classes, completed all the coursework, and passed all the tests in the two years.

Most days, Enrique was able to drive Anay the three miles to school and pick her up at 8:30 each night. However, there were many days when there was no car, or the car was not working, and Anay had to take the bus. This required her to leave the school a little early and walk three blocks to the bus stop to catch the last bus of the evening. If she missed that bus, she walked the three miles in the dark down a busy highway to the alley that led to her neighborhood. Enrique waited for her at the entrance to the alley to walk her the last few blocks. One December, their car had starter trouble (among other problems). Anay told me with a smile, "Enrique and Kiké would get in the car, and the girls and I would push and push until he got it started. Then we hopped in and we went."

GRADUATION

Anay graduated from her high school in August 2008. Valle Alta held a formal graduation ceremony and steak dinner at the Holiday Inn in Ciudad Juárez. Anay saved and borrowed enough money to purchase eight tickets, each costing twenty-five dollars, so that Enrique, the children, my husband, and I could attend. We met them in the hotel parking lot. Anay got out of the car dressed most elegantly in a black taffeta cocktail dress with a silver-sequined cummerbund and strappy black heels. Her hair was up and her makeup was perfect. In my familiarity, I had not realized how beautiful she is.

But the girls! Each of them had on a princess dress. The dresses were in shades of creamy to yellow satin, not the same, but similar in color and style. Each had a bodice of sequins and pearls with long flowing skirts—not the play princess dresses you can buy at Walmart. They were made to fit each girl perfectly. Somehow, Anay found three pairs of little plastic heels that looked like glass slippers. The transparent wedge heels were filled with water with colorful toy fish and glitter floating inside. They wore their hair pinned and sprayed in curly up-dos. They wore identical gaudy plastic jeweled necklaces, the kind of bling in the dollar stores that catches a little girl's eye. My husband and I held their hands in dance motion and spun them around so the skirts billowed out while we sang, "Look at the lovely princess dancing." They couldn't stop grinning and prancing. Little Enrique came out of the car in a satiny green vest and dress pants, wanting to get to spin around also. I spun him like an airplane, and he squealed and loudly demanded more.

Last to come out of the car was Anay's mother, Ofelia. This was the first time I had ever met her. I held back my gasp as I saw how much Anay resembled her mother. I greeted her warmly, but she was a little reserved. I think she had heard many stories about the strange woman from over the border and her role in her daughter's life, and she was not sure how to react.

We encountered trouble when we walked to the door to show our tickets. The manager of the school, Fernie, met Anay and said that the children could not enter, and that she had to buy one more ticket. He was so sorry, but the hotel policy was that there could be no children. He told me, in broken English, "There is just no more room, no room for children. We are so full. All the tables are full. It is the hotel rule."

I told Anay that my husband and I could wait in the hotel lobby with the girls while she, Enrique, and her mother attended the ceremony. She said, "No, we'll be okay." Then she disappeared with another woman who was standing near the ticket table. We waited outside, unsure what to do. I was worried that they didn't have the money to buy the ticket. I mentioned quietly to Enrique, "Do you need more money?" He said to just wait.

Soon, Anay said for us to follow her inside. A woman met us at a table in the corner. The round tables were set for ten, with elegant chair covers and centerpieces. The woman explained, "There is room for you and three of the children at this table. We will move this extra chair in. But one adult and one child will need to sit at that table over there." Ofelia and I sat side-by-side, Eva and Juliet sat between me and my husband, and Elaine sat on my lap. Enrique and little Enrique went to the other table. Anay joined the graduates outside. I was lost in all the conversations about the mix-up with the tickets, and thought it best not to discuss it any more in this setting.

Ofelia and I chatted just a little before the ceremony began.

"I enjoyed meeting your family in southern Mexico and seeing the beautiful land. Very different from Juárez, no?"

"It is beautiful. I am going back there."

"Really, you'll move back?"

"Yes, very soon."

"Well, maybe it is safer than Juárez. Isn't Anay beautiful tonight?"

She didn't hear that comment, or else ignored it. "You know, I never got to go to school. I work in the maquiladora now. I have to stand up all day long making the harnesses. It's so hard. I have trouble with my legs. I want to leave."

I was not sure how to interpret this comment, but maybe she wanted me to explore deeper into the hardships she endured as a maquiladora employee. Our conversation ended as the ceremony began. It was set for 7:30 but started at 8:00 with the presentation of the national Mexican flag, the pledge with arms extended toward the flag, and singing of the Mexican national anthem.

The school is small. There was a morning graduating class of thirty students, and an evening graduating class, Anay's group, of thirty-six students. The morning group marched in as the master of ceremonies announced the school name and the class name while a keyboard musician played a classic march; then the evening class marched in when its name was called. All were wearing deep green caps and gowns. The woman who had found seating for us made an opening speech. She was Carla Luján, the founder and owner of the school. The mayor was listed on the agenda as the next speaker, but he was not in attendance. We clapped for this year's outstanding teacher, who made a short speech. Four students performed a traditional Mexican dance to a CD played on a portable player. Since we were near the back wall, the little girls got up to dance to the music and spin around in their pretty dresses. When the music stopped and the speeches began, five-year-old Juliet sat on my lap. I provided paper and a marker to keep her busy. I noticed that she had drawn five starbursts by crisscrossing lines so that they all met in the middle. Four of the starbursts were small and one was large. I asked her what these were. "This one is me, this one is Elaine, that one is Eva, and that one is Kiké. And *that* star [she pointed to the large one], that one is my mama."

Next on the agenda, awards were given. Two students in each group received top honors. Anay was one of the awardees for the evening class. We clapped and cheered when her name was called, and we held the children up so they could see over the crowd as she made her way to the podium to receive her certificate. Each graduate came forward when his or her name was called to receive a diploma. The school director declared the graduates official; they threw their caps in the air and dispersed for group and family photographs. We met by the pool and took many photos of friends, family, gowns, and pretty dresses. Then they called us in to eat.

Anay joined us, and we started joking a little with the family who shared our table as we passed around the basket of bread and butter. The hotel served each of the children a plate of chicken nuggets, gave each of the adults a salad, and set a bottomless pitcher of Coke on the table. We were all thirsty, so I poured half a glass of Coke for everyone at the table. The waiter quickly took the empty pitcher and gave us a full one. I know Anay doesn't let the girls have Coke, but this was special, and there was no alternative. I did monitor how much they drank. Soon the waiters brought out a plate of baked potato and steak for each of us. The steak was so large it extended over the edge of the plate. They served us slowly . . . one plate here, another one there. My husband and I were afraid that one or more of us might need to share a plate, but soon we all had more than we could possibly eat.

After a little more Mexican music and students' dancing, the mariachis came out to provide more professional entertainment, and the festivities became less formal and more celebratory. The little girls danced even more, and we pulled little Kiké out from under more than one table full of strangers. It was late, Anay's mother was with them, and we had a long drive home. So we hugged and kissed and congratulated all around and left. I had many questions to ask Anay about the evening, but they had to wait.

REFLECTING ON THE BIG DAY

A few days later, the family drove into El Paso and we agreed to meet. Peter Piper Pizza is our best spot. The children play games with Enrique, and Anay and I get to visit.

"You know, I had asked my mother if she wanted to come to my graduation. She said, 'Why would I want to go to that?!' So, I didn't get her a ticket. Then, that night, she showed up at our house saying she was going! So, Enrique whispered to me that it was okay, he would just stay outside so she could go in. But it worked out. That Fernie! Never did they tell me that the kids could not go. I bought them tickets. They *had* to see my graduation. We were all in this together. You saw my teacher. She was at the ticket line. She saw what Fernie was saying. She took me back to the owner of the school and told her. That is when they let us in. Fernie is just like that. He wants to have so many rules. He was lying. He said there was not room, and there *was* room for the kids! You know, he told me that if I went with you on that trip to my home and missed some school, I could not get that award for outstanding graduate. So I told him, okay, but I was going on that trip. But the owner gave it to me anyway. I didn't know that I would get that award."

I asked where she got those beautiful dresses.

"There is this very nice older lady, Doña Rosa. I met her one day when we were waiting and waiting so long at a clinic to see the doctor. She was so lonely. She used to have some money when her daughter was younger, so her daughter had some pretty dresses for her *quinceañera* [coming-out party for a fifteen-year-old girl] and her graduations. But now, they were just thrown in a box. Her husband left her when her daughter got married. Now she is all alone and doesn't have much. Enrique and I would take her food and visit with her. I would massage her neck and shoulders. She loved it when I rubbed her head right here [pointing to her temple]. It would make her relax.

"So, she told me that I could have those dresses. I started at four o'clock the day before and I worked until one in the morning on those dresses. The girls' dresses were all from the daughter of this little old lady. But she was fat! So I had to cut and cut and remake them. That neighbor, you know, the one who is Indian? She helped me cut the dresses down to the right size. But I sewed them all with just needle and thread. And Enrique had to work that night, so it was just me and all the kids! But, I did it!

"My dress, did you see? That sequined belt? It was a sleeve that I took off of a dress someone gave us in a bag of clothes. I made it into a belt. The top was from another dress that came in one of the bags. All of my friends at school said it was a pretty dress, and they couldn't believe how I made it."

Anay was serious about continuing her education at the college level. The university in Ciudad Juárez allowed freshmen to enroll only if they had completed their high school work in May. Anay's school was year-round, and she finished in August. This left her with one more setback—a wait of many months before she could even apply to the university.

OTHER STUDENTS AT VALLE ALTA

I visited Valle Alta high school several times. It is tucked in a sandy alley way behind a shopping center. The building was U-shaped, with the main entrance and offices at the top of the U and two stories of classrooms above the office and extending the legs of the U. The bottom of the U was closed off with a block wall, and a concrete open area and basketball court filled the center of the U. The walls were made of the concrete blocks that are so common in Mexico. The building was well maintained and adequately furnished.

The director allowed my graduate students from the University of Texas at El Paso to interview some of the other students in the evening school. With their help, we gathered information about these nontraditional high school students. Below are short profiles of some of Anay's classmates to illuminate where high school education fits into the life options of these maquiladora workers.[1] The names are pseudonyms.

EDUARDO

"I dropped out of school when I was sixteen so I could work in a maquiladora to help my family. I work at the same maquiladora as my father. He is right over there [he pointed to another student]. Now we are finishing high school together. We worked in the maquiladora all day, and then we repair cars in the evenings and weekends. My father told me to quit the maquiladora job so I can study hard and do well in school. So now I just go to school and repair cars. As soon as I graduate, I am going to the university here. Then I can be a manager or supervisor at a maquiladora. They want my dad to learn English so he can help the visitors when they come to the plant. So, he studies hard, but he doesn't get to spend very much time with our family. I know it's hard for him."

MARSELA

"I can read and write English. I used to live in New Mexico, and I went to school there. That's why. But, they deported me a few years ago. I don't think it was right how they did it. I really want to be a lawyer and study immigration law. I have four children, two boys and two girls. And I take care of my elderly parents. So I really want to go to law school and have a career to take care of all of them. Now I am taking these classes: math, physics, chemistry, economics, and history.

"Do you know anything about immigration law? On my own, I study the 1930 Immigration Law. I read everything I can about it. I want to know how it has changed in this past century. I want to know a lot about the rights that immigrants have in the United States."

VIRGINIA

"Well, I am nineteen. There are six children in our family, and I am the baby. I live at home with my mother and father. Everyone else is married and has children, but I do not want to get married or have any children anytime soon! I don't even have time to go out with my friends . . . well, a little on the weekends. So, I am the only one who went to school beyond elementary school. I have been here at Valle Alta for two years, and I will graduate in April. I work full time at the Davol maquiladora here in Juárez, and they pay for me to come to this school.

"I saw my brothers and sisters struggle so hard with money for their families and all the fighting and divorces. I want a life that is different from that. I want a job that will pay well. Already, the maquiladora gave me two raises because I am here at school. I have more responsibility at work now, too. And I really like it.

"But it is hard. If I am sick or don't come to school for some reason and miss an exam, I have to pay [the equivalent of thirty dollars] to the school to get to take that exam. Sometimes the maquiladora keeps me late, and I can't get a ride here to the school in time. The school here is really nice. If it is the maquiladora's fault, they won't make me pay for the test.

"This is really hard. I have to get up at 4:30 in the morning to dress and catch my bus to the maquiladora. Then I come here right after work. I don't get home until about 9:30. And I have to hurry to get out of here by 8:20 so I don't miss the last bus. Then I have homework. I am always so tired.

"I'm not sure what I'll do next. If I can go to university, I want to study psychology and maybe open up my own practice. But I don't know how I can pay for that. So, maybe I'll just stay working at the maquiladora. My sister lives in the United States. She said maybe I could go live with her. I don't know. We'll see."

ALBERTO

"Whew! Give me just a minute. I'm out of breath from shooting hoops in the break . . . Okay, now I'm ready. I'm really not from Juárez. I am from Michoacán. It is a beautiful state, not dry like here. But my father came here to take a better job. I came to this school because it is so close to my house, and they accepted all my credits from my school in Michoacán. The other schools would not take those credits. Yes, I do work in a maquiladora and I referee soccer games on the weekends. That is what I love to do. I will finish in April. I am going to the Universidad Autónoma de Chihuahua in Juárez to study kinesiology and athletic training. I have a girlfriend, but we are not going to get married until we both finish university. Do you know that I started as a janitor and now I am a receptionist?"

LOUISA

"Well, yes, I was born here in Juárez. I have four children, and no husband. My maquiladora is paying for me to come to school. I get paid more than the line workers. I hope that I can get a higher salary so I can be with my children. [She broke down and sobbed. After a minute she was able to continue.] They have to go to a boarding school for poor children. I take them to the school on Sunday night and do not see them again until I pick them up on Friday night.

"Go to university! Ha! I want nothing more than to have a better life for my children, and the only way to achieve this goal is to finish my high school education. I always wanted to be a nurse. But it's not my choice. Who would finance my education? The maquiladora won't finance that . . . it is of no use to them."

LORENZO

"I am one of three children. My parents are hard working. They only got a primary education, but they continually encouraged us to get our education. But when I entered *secundaria*, I had to drop out. We could not afford it. That is what my brothers did. We all dropped out so we could work and help the family.

"I was great in science, but not so good in mathematics. I have been working at Kentucky Fried Chicken since then. I have gone up the ladder and progressed with that company throughout these years. But that is all I could do without more education. When I finish high school, they say I will have more opportunities. Maybe I can.

"Really, I want to be a genetic engineer and open a company. I do need to know English better. I hope my little brother will not drop out of *secundaria*, that he'll go on to high school."

ANNA

"No, I am not from here. I'm from Durango. But there were no jobs there. My father is a truck driver. But my parents couldn't live here, so they returned to Durango. I work at Davol, like many of the people here. These are the only people I know, my friends here and at Davol. I've been there two years.

"You want to know what I get paid? Okay. I get 3,120 pesos per month [about 290 dollars]. That includes stamps to buy my lunch at the cafeteria. The shift is Monday through Saturday, 6:30 A.M. to 3:50 P.M. with a ten-minute break in the morning and a thirty-minute lunch break.

"So, I live with my friend. She works in the same maquiladora and goes to this school also. We have a little one-room apartment, and we pay 800 pesos [about 64 dollars], but we have to pay utility bills also. I would like to go to university and study criminal justice, but I just don't see that I can afford it, and we don't have any government help for that."

INTERPRETIVE CONTEXT:
HIGH SCHOOLS IN CIUDAD JUÁREZ

Education provided some degree of hope for these students. Unknown to us are the endings to their stories. The downturn in the U.S. economy in 2008 was strongly felt in Ciudad Juárez as factories and other businesses closed their doors. Those factories that remained open put many of their employees on half-time work schedules. At this writing, Davol Surgical Innovations was still open, and perhaps the need for surgical instruments will remain strong and those who were promised advancement at the factory upon graduation from high school may receive that. Their hopes for university education, like Anay's, depend entirely on outside funding. Friends in the United States, a family that pools all its resources to support one child, or a rare government grant seem to be the only options to provide the financial resources for a university education. Although university education is free (but difficult to gain admittance) in some places in Mexico, it is not so in Ciudad Juárez. In fact, the costs are not much lower than the average U.S. state-school tuition.

Some elaboration on high schools in Mexico follows. These programs vary greatly, so my comments are limited to the schools that I have visited in Ciudad Juárez. In the United States most high schools are public. In Mexico most are private, like Valle Alta, and they include grades ten through twelve. Government funds may be available via scholarships and special funding programs. There are two main kinds of Mexican high schools. One, the *preparatoria*, provides a general curriculum to prepare for further education. The *bachillerato* schools provide a more vocational curriculum that may be structured as two- or three-year programs. Valle Alta high school was unusual in that its fees were reasonable and the schedule made education available to those who worked in the daytime. More often, students compete for the few seats in a private high school that charges much higher fees. I credit Carla Luján for her contributions to Mexican education at reduced financial gain to her business.

I have visited another high school in the city, which we will call Preparatoria Buenavista. It has a similar open-access approach, although it does not have evening classes. The administrator of this school, Armida Valdez, was an activist in trying to maintain an open curriculum that was rich in humanities and offered varied opportunities for the students. When I first visited the school in 2001, the menu of class options was lengthy and included classes for pre-med, border arts, political science, communications, and theater. The communications students participated in a class in critical journalism in which they wrote a newspaper about local events. Their reports told the news from the viewpoint of people in their community, often in contrast to the official reporting of the media.

With government-mandated curriculum reform in 2003, the school was required to reduce its menu to twelve mandatory courses—all in such business-related subjects as business machines, economics, business management, and accounting. This business-prep curriculum served well the needs of factories and those students who wanted to enter private business. However, the state mandate greatly reduced the rich and varied curriculum that Buenavista had previously provided. Ms. Valdez gathered the principals of six other high schools, and together they visited the government education office to petition against the change, but their petition was denied. Government education officials visited the schools each year to verify that the business curriculum was being implemented. Prior to this dictate, the students at Preparatoria Buenavista had exposure to a wide variety of subjects that would allow them to consider a variety of careers. After the mandate, all students were exposed to a prescribed curriculum for business career preparation.

These issues of access and curriculum quality are not unique to Mexico. In many communities in the United States, more than 40 percent (Green and Winters, 2005) of students do not graduate from high school. In addition, studies show us that because of accountability policies and standards, the education students receive in U.S. high schools is often reduced to that of a teach-to-the-test curriculum (McNeil, 2000; Valenzuela, 2004). We do find excellent examples of access and quality in pockets throughout both countries, but there is much room for improvement.

The strong government support to education in the United States provides access to secondary school, including transportation, for almost all students. What might happen to that access if the nation moves to more private educational enterprises as we see in Mexico?

| SIX |

Maquiladoras and Violence

THE LINE WORKERS

In the early years of our research collaboration, Anay, Enrique, and I visited many communities on the outskirts of Ciudad Juárez, communities that had sprung up in the past few years to accommodate the 250,000 maquiladora employees. Virtually every member of these communities had recently moved to the city from the interior of Mexico, and when we met them, they were living in temporary houses, most of which were made with cast-off materials. We saw many a house, often no more than a shelter, with a particle board roof held down with old tires to counter the forces of spring winds, and some with fences made of mattress springs, car hoods, or packing pallets. Most of these families struggled to survive with only one source of income—the salary of the one or two family members who worked on the assembly lines in the maquiladora—about two hundred dollars per person per month. We walked down the sandy unpaved roads and encountered people outside busy with chores such as hanging their clothes on a fence or a makeshift clothesline or boiling water on an outside fire. We chatted with the people and gained more insight into their worlds. Each family brought different experiences to this large, desert cauldron. We tell a few of their stories below to highlight some typical experiences of individuals who came to the border to work in these factories. (The names are pseudonyms.)

Karla, at thirty-five, was a single mother of four who had recently moved into a small house with her sister's family because she had separated from her husband. She moved to Ciudad Juárez about ten years earlier from Gómez Palacio, Durango. When we met her, she and her sister's teenage daughter were washing clothes in an electric washing machine outside of the small block house and hanging the clothes on a line. The two youngest children, ages three and eight, were outside with them. The house consisted of four small rooms and a tiny bathroom. Eight people were living there.

Karla had worked in the maquiladoras for ten years, and her latest job was making vacuum cleaners at the Electrolux plant. "I really don't like the job—the same thing all day long. I make about sixty pesos [about US$5.50] a day, but they take out forty pesos [about US$3.50] each week for my lunch. The good thing is that I have social security with this job so I can get free health care. Some maquiladoras have a clinic on the site, but mine doesn't. The kids stay here and someone in the family watches them while I work. They do have a place where the kids can stay at the factory, but it is *muy tirado* [trashy], ugh! I wouldn't leave my children there."

As mentioned earlier, a big problem for laborers in Ciudad Juárez is transportation. Hundreds of old buses run continually in the city to provide transportation from pickup points to the maquiladoras. The rides often take one hour or more. The pickup points are not very close to most employees' homes. Women are particularly vulnerable to the isolation and exposure that this dependence on the bus services creates—especially in this era of feminicide in the city.

For Karla this commute was particularly difficult. After a forty-minute ride, the first bus let her off at a place where she had to catch a second bus that brought her closer to her neighborhood. Then she had to walk several long blocks on the sandy street to reach her sister's house, where she and the two children were living. Because her shift ended after midnight, she arrived at the bus stop in the early morning darkness. A house belonging to a different sister was nearer to this second bus stop, so for safety she stayed in that house for the rest of the night. She got up early each morning and walked home, usually arriving about 6:30. Then she played with the children, got them to school, and slept most of the morning. Although she was separated from her husband, he came to help with the children for a few hours while she was at work in the evenings. She said she hoped to move to a maquiladora that was closer to her home. However, since many factories had shut down or left the city in response to the U.S. economic downturn, finding a different maquiladora job would be difficult.

Twenty-eight-year-old Marcos came from the state of Veracruz to work on a farm in Texas as an illegal employee. Immigration officers caught him and he was deported, leaving behind his pregnant wife who was a U.S. citizen. He has never returned to the United States and, as a consequence, has never seen the baby. When I met him, he was a line worker for one of the several factories making harnesses for electronic components for the auto industry. He had been working at this job for two years. Marcos began work at 6:15 in the morning and ended at 3:45 in the afternoon, with a twenty-minute break for lunch. He usually ate food he brought from home and sometimes purchased fruit or bread from the dining area. The maquiladora provided a lunch, but he said it was the same food every day and the quantity was not sufficient. He told me he earned the equivalent of about six dollars per day, the same salary he started with two years ago. He walked to work and back, about one mile each way, to his home—a small room in a Christian church building provided in exchange for serving as the guard and maintenance man for the church. There was a bathroom in the church that he was allowed to use and a kitchen that he was not allowed to use because the women reserved it for their church events.

"My mother still lives in Veracruz, but she is in poor health. I send money to her every month. In her last letter, she wrote that her teeth are hurting. I was saving money to go home to see her, but now I think I will send her the money to go to the dentist." A few older individuals in Mexico have a pension and health care, but most do not. They depend on their children as Marcos's mother does.

Enrique also worked in the maquiladoras off and on for several years and described this work environment: "I worked in the maquiladoras for several years before I got my preacher's certificate and got a job as a missionary. I was five years working at the maquiladora that made plastic pieces for cars. My job was to work the machine that ground the plastic edges off. That made so much dust. They didn't give me anything to protect my breathing, and that fine dust was all around me all day. The cleaner was like a vacuum cleaner that sucked the air. We had to clean all the dust out of that machine.

"Then I quit that job, but sometimes we had to have more money than the church paid me, so I worked in the candy factories at night. My job there was also to clean the machine where the candy went into bags. Some of these bags were for Walmart and some were for, I think, Great Value. There was candy dust flying all around in those factories also. I was breathing that all day. I had to stop working there because my eyes were always red and watery, my nose always had green mucus, and I had a cough all the time. The doctor says I still have chronic allergies. And I have headaches all the time.

"My brother-in-law, Javier, works in the maquiladora Strawberry [the name of a candy factory]. He says it is not very clean there. We know a young woman who works with him and she has serious health problems breathing through her nose. Maybe she has lead or blood in her nose."

A teaching colleague of mine, Alejandro Medina, shares this experience: "Since I was getting my industrial engineering degree, I wanted to know what it was like from the ground up. So I took a job at a maquiladora—a smaller Mexican factory. I arrived very early each day so they would not know that I had a car. I wanted them to think I was just a regular worker. My job was to cut out metal pieces. I worked three hours cutting, moving that heavy cutting press over and over for three hours with no break. Then they changed me to a huge drill, which was also hard physical labor. Those are big machines and very dangerous. And you just do that over and over. It is really boring and hard. I worked fifty hours that week and they paid me a little over fifty dollars because I got a bonus for being on time . . . fifty dollars for the whole week! I took my girlfriend to the fair that weekend, and it was all gone . . . a week's pay. That was hard work. I am young and healthy, but I was so tired when I got home. My friends called me to play football, but I just went to bed. I didn't last very long at that job. I don't know how they do it day after day."

One employee who earned about ten dollars per day described to us his weekly expenses: eleven dollars for drinking water, five dollars to rent an abandoned bus as the family home, twenty dollars for electricity, and ten dollars for transportation by bus or taxi. His wife earned about the same amount, the majority of which was spent on groceries.

The maquiladora employment structure and low wages affect living conditions for thousands of individuals in communities and neighborhoods similar to the one where Anay and Enrique lived. These people struggle just to attain the necessities, living over a social safety net that is full of holes. The federal government does provide medical services to the employees and their families, although access is limited. The maquiladoras, off and on according to their need for labor, provide some services such as home loans and educational support. And some of the employees have achieved a relatively comfortable lifestyle—they can purchase the food they need, share a car, and slowly begin to improve their small homes by replacing the temporary building materials with concrete block. This comfort level is fragile and can be upended by factors such as poor health, unexpected pregnancy, car trouble, or an accident. Those who find some stability depend on advantages that are usually outside the norm— two or more members of the family are steadily employed, the family has external support from extended family for child care, everyone stays healthy, and, for the fortunate ones, there is a little support from family or friends in the United States. However, even those small success stories were threatened in 2009, as the economic downturn caused in part by the housing loan collapse in the United States added another set of hardships for these employees and their neighbors. The stress in their lives escalated to extreme levels when drug-related violence in the city soared. Anay's experiences working in a maquiladora and living in the maquiladora community provide a graphic gateway to understanding the violence and its escalation.

THE MASK AND THE YELLOW EYES

Anay was sixteen in 1999 when she began work in the maquiladora. She worked long hours, 7:00 A.M. to 7:00 P.M., six days a week, to get the overtime pay that was offered at that time. After a few months, the factory cut back on overtime opportunities, relegating her to the 6:00 A.M. to 3:00 P.M. shift. She received the equivalent of about seventy dollars per week with the overtime work and about fifty dollars per week without the overtime. She paid rent to her mother and helped pay the family's gasoline bills.

"I could walk from the maquiladora to the house, but it took about an hour, so usually I took the *ruta* [maquiladora bus]. But on the days I stayed late for my school, I had to take a different *ruta*, and I had to wait a long time for that one. I stayed at the maquiladora in the afternoons, yes, about 3:00 to 5:00, on three days a week. Well, those days changed if the tutor could come or not. That tutor worked with us in the school. We were working on the *secundaria* books.

"Sometimes I got out late. After six, there is no bus at the maquiladora. That night, I went with my friend to catch a different bus. I still had on my apron from work. And I had my book bag. I went with her, and she caught her bus. I waited for mine. It was late. I didn't know anything about the women murders. There were many cars passing by. A man in a truck came by and wanted me to get up in the truck. He knew my name. I just stayed there not looking at him. He got out and grabbed at me.

There was this large light pole. I grabbed that pole and hugged it so tight. He couldn't pull me. He had this handkerchief over his nose and a white hat. I remember his eyes . . . yellow, yellow like a white person, right here, under his eyebrows. I remember the black pickup truck and the shiny, new tires. I thought someone would help me. I was crying and screaming and holding onto that pole. Finally, he just grabbed my book bag and took off.

"The Del Río [a popular convenience store] was right there and I went in and someone called the police from there. The police came and said there is nothing they can do. My mom said it was my fault for being alone, and I should just go on the bus and not wait for school.

"I went the next day and told the people at the maquiladora. The woman in Human Resources called me, and I told her that I knew those yellow eyes. I think I had seen them at the maquiladora. She said she couldn't help me.

"And, get this, after one month, it happened again! This truck was white. He called my name also. I think it was the same man. This man I know from Del Río saved me. He came running out at that guy. The man had a gun, but I don't think it had bullets. He used the gun to hit my friend in the head. I took off running into the store. The guy drove away. You know, he had the same handkerchief, the same hat, and those same yellow eyes. I think the license plate for that truck was from El Paso."

One of the families that Anay and Enrique know through their church had a teenage daughter in Enrique's youth group. Her name was Lydia. I remembered her from one of my visits to their church because she loved to sing, and she sang very loudly in the church services, mostly off-key, but with gusto. Enrique shared this story about Lydia.

"Do you remember Lydia, the one from church that sang loud? She disappeared one day when walking home from working in the maquiladora. About three weeks later, her body was found in a vacant lot on the west side of the city. She was raped. Her legs were both broken. It looked like someone beat her legs with a metal pipe. Her mother always cries; she cannot stop crying."

THE FEMINICIDES

As documented in the introduction to this book, in the early years of the maquiladora industry the factories hired mostly women, for several reasons. Women were perceived as less inclined to unionize and a little more stable as they had fewer occupational choices. This created a shockwave in a society where men's and women's roles had been clearly defined for generations. A woman's independence or a man's dependence on her income constituted an alarming social intrusion and contributed to more tremors in the family and social structures. Moreover, the maquiladora-sponsored influx of laborers from the interior of the country to the border further altered the ratio of men to women. Norma Iglesias Prieto's work documents this phenomenon (1997, p. xix).

> The hiring of women, while it has generated employment, has failed to offer even a partial solution to the overall problem of unemployment and underemployment in the border region. Throughout the region maquiladoras typically have employed a labor force that is 80 to 90 percent female. This fundamental characteristic has affected the occupational structure and socioculture character of border cities as it has the families of female workers.

The violence erupts in several ways. In the early years of the 2000s, gang rivalry over the control of the drug industry that supplies the lucrative and almost bottomless U.S. market for illegal drugs exploded. Mexican border cities bear most of the brunt of the violent action. Men are murdered at even higher rates, but the manner in which women are murdered is particularly brutal. In some segments of society, especially near the border, women are demonized and victimized, especially if they work in the maquiladoras or if they visit bars. These are bold women who step over the traditional lines. Most likely, this attitude toward working women has contributed to the ongoing murders of women in the city and the lack of investigation and prosecution of the criminals. Almost four hundred women were murdered between 1993 and 2003, and it continues today at almost the same rate: about thirty murders per year. Few of these murders, if any, have been investigated or solved. The murders, early on, were called the Maquiladora Murders, because many victims were young women who worked in the factories. Today, most any female could become the next casualty. Many of the women murdered in Ciudad Juárez have been mutilated or raped. Several bodies discovered in the desert display the same torture patterns; as one account of the vicious crimes attests, the right nipple has been bitten off, and the left breast has been cut off (Washington Valdez, 2006).

Drugs, gangs, corruption, and domestic violence are credited as causes for these murders (Rodríguez and Montané, 2007). Molloy and Bowden (2011) interviewed one of the major assassins involved in the cartel violence in the city. He had given up his life of crime after his conversion to Christianity and is presently hiding in another country. He reported that one of his roles in the cartel was to find attractive girls on the street in Ciudad Juárez and tell them that he would take them to a party where they would receive gifts. These girls ended up being used sexually by the drug bosses. Some stayed on as "wives," meaning they chose to comply rather than to die. Nevertheless, sooner or later, most were murdered.

Rodríguez and Montané's 2007 book, *The Daughters of Juárez: A True Story of Serial Murders South of the Border*, provides evidence obtained from their interviews with families affected by the feminicides. These victims' relatives often condemned the police for their involvement in the rapes and murders. In case after case, when their daughter disappeared, the frantic parents reported the event to the police, only to be met with flippant remarks effectively blaming the victim. The authors detail several instances in which the girls were wearing jeans and their maquiladora work apron, yet the families were told that it was the daughter's fault for dressing in short skirts. Common responses were, "Your daughter just went off with her boyfriend," or, "She was leading a separate life working the bars.

You didn't really know her." The parents stated that the police would file a report but would not contact the parents again until a body was found. Often when the police did take action, they committed purposeful errors that strangled any hope of solving the crime. In addition to blaming the victim and failing to keep the families informed, according to Rodríguez and Montané's documentation, police not only bungled investigations but also grossly contaminated crime scenes; clothing and other evidence were left at the scene, lost, or burned, and few if any records with vital evidence such as DNA were created. Parents were notified about a decomposed body with some physical characteristic of their daughter's. They were left to bury someone's child and wait in the hell of the unknown.

Rodríguez and Montané go on to tell the story of María Talamantes. María was arrested when a neighbor started a fight with her family. While in the holding cell, she was drugged and gang-raped by the police. One of the policemen showed her a scrapbook of pictures of policemen raping, torturing, and killing girls and young women. In spite of threats from these police officers, she took the case to trial and provided a very plausible account of the rape. Predictably, it was dismissed for "lack of evidence." María Talamantes reported to the authors that when she returned to work at the maquiladora, she saw one of the same policemen, one of her rapists, serving as a security guard.

Diana Washington Valdez (2006), a reporter for the *El Paso Times*, has spent a great part of her career reporting on this ghastly phenomenon, and she has paid the cost in emotional stress and threats to her life. Her writings illustrate the connections between the business and political leaders of the city and the murders. Her book, *Harvest of Women: Safari in Mexico*, provides additional and detailed documentation of many of the murders, highlighting the appalling experiences that the families of the victims encountered when dealing with the authorities.

> Over the years, the cases were characterized by a lack of true investigation, a disregard for victims and their families, the

arrests of suspects whose guilt was doubtful, intimidation and threats against advocacy groups, and the official bungling and corruption that permitted the slayings to continue (59).

THE VIOLENT CITY

Yet, these brutal feminicides are only a fraction of the city's violence. Molly Molloy's Frontera List (http://groups.google.com /group/frontera-list) provides reports of the numbers of people killed daily along with monthly totals. More than 1,600 people were murdered in 2008, about 2,700 in 2009, and more than 3,000 in 2010. Anay's individual recollections add more spine-chilling details. In the few months that Anay's family lived in Ciudad Juárez in 2008, the violence crept dangerously close to the family. We will start the ghastly experiences with Anay's account of the brutal murder of a good friend.

"There was this good friend of ours, Alberto Bernal. He and his wife used to live here in our neighborhood. They were very humble, and always helping us. They were like our family. He was killed last week! We went to the funeral and cried and cried! He got a good job working at the prison. He was a good worker and so honest that he kept getting better jobs and better jobs. So, he had a good salary, so they moved into a better house closer to the prison.

"His wife said that some guys came to him a few weeks ago and said, 'Take these drugs into the prison. You can have some of the money if you do.' He covered his eyes so that he did not see them and he said, 'I can't do that. I am proud of my honesty. But, don't worry. I didn't ever see you, and I don't even know you. I'll never say anything.'

"Two days later, he was found sitting in his pick up on Zaragosa Street where it crosses Juan Gabriel near that big Soriana Store. The door was open and he had a bullet through his chest, right here [she pointed to her sternum]. We are still so sad. We just went to his funeral. Everyone was crying so much."

Just three weeks after Mr. Bernal's death, Anay called me sobbing.

"I can't stop crying. I cried all night, and I am still shaking. Last night I was coming home from the school. I caught the bus there by S-Mart because I had to get some eggs and beans and tortillas to feed the kids. So, our bus was driving on that street and there is this drug rehabilitation house. Some of the men and a priest were sitting outside on the sidewalk. Our bus was right there when these four men dressed in black with masks and rifles jumped out of a truck and started shooting them. There was blood all over the sidewalk, and some of the men were dead on the sidewalk. We were so scared in the bus. We told that driver, 'Get out of here! Get out of here!' He said no because those guys would see him. We said he better get out of there quick or they would start shooting us. Finally he took off. It was so awful!"

The violence draws in many unwilling individuals as it attempted to draw in Mr. Bernal. He had to make the choice to participate in the prison drug business or risk his life. He chose the honest route that cost him his life.

The large gangs often insist that business owners pay them monthly protection fees. In reality, this means that the gangs will not damage the business. To reject this mob-type extortion would likely result in the businesses' being vandalized or even burned down by their would-be "protectors." To accept the agreement, on the other hand, puts the owners under gang control and simultaneously makes them a target for competing gangs.

Enrique's nephew was drawn into the violence. "My nephew, Gerardo, is in prison for selling drugs, but it is not really fair. Yes, he should not be selling drugs, but the punishment is not right. See, he used to work with his dad, my brother, making houses. A few years ago, the government was building a lot of houses for the people in Juárez, so they could work in construction. They got 1,500 pesos a week [about US$120], and that was a good salary. So, he got married and they had a baby. Then everyone lost their jobs when the economy went down. He was six months without work with a wife and baby to take care of. One of his friends said, 'Come on, you can get 1,000 pesos [about US$90] in just two days with this guy and the marijuana.' So he decided to do it. He lied to his dad and said he had a job building a private house. He just worked about a week with that guy. That Saturday, he left early with his backpack. He and his friend were going to this warehouse with some other kids. There, they were packing marijuana into bricks. He had done this one other day. At ten that morning, soldiers broke in and arrested the three guys, including Gerardo. He told the judge the truth, that he had only been doing that one week. The judge said it didn't matter how long. And the judge said that he probably was the leader of this group of narcos. Gerardo said to the judge, 'Look at me and my clothes and shoes. Does this look like I am rich?' But they put him in prison. One of the gangsters came to Gerardo and the other two guys. Well, one was about thirty years old. They just let him out of jail! So he was probably in with the judge somehow. But Gerardo and the other kid—the gangster got them together and said that one of them had to confess that he was the leader of that group at the warehouse and that those were all his drugs. So, this way, the police would never look for the real narco trafficker. Then they would close the case. The other kid did not have a family, so they told him that he had to confess to that. If not, they would kill both of them in prison. But Gerardo was in that jail for fifteen days before he saw the judge. The prison guards tortured him and the other kid. They put electric wires on their testicles and beat them right under the arms on the ribs. That is when the other kid had to sign that he was the owner of the marijuana warehouse. Finally, after fifteen days, Gerardo's mother got to see him in jail. He showed her the bruises where they tortured him. But he has to stay in prison for seven years."

Enrique's nephew is an example of a *nini*. This term shows up frequently in studies of the social problems in Ciudad Juárez, and it comes from the phrase "*Ni trabajo, ni escuela*," which means "neither work nor school." There are large numbers of young people in the city between the ages of fifteen and twenty-five who are not working and are not in school. In essence, then, this vacuum in their social and economic lives ends up sucking in trouble.

When the violence oozed into Anay and Enrique's neighborhood, we became very concerned. To get to their house, you have to make a sharp turn into a narrow, rutted lane between a school and a junk car dealership. For a while, some teenage boys would hover over that entrance, flashing knives. When a car slowed down to enter the neighborhood, the boys would rob the people in the car. The youths left after a few days, perhaps realizing that it was not a very lucrative business corner.

Anay shared another grave story. "You know, we see this shiny new red pickup truck in our neighborhood now. They stop by that neighbor's house where she has a little store in her living room. One of our neighbors said that she went to the store with her kid. Someone was in front of them at the store buying sugar. That lady handed them a bag of sugar. The guy shook his head, 'No.' Then the lady gave them a bag of sugar in a brown wrapper! Sugar! Right! I know that that truck is bringing cocaine to sell in that store! It is getting dangerous here."

One time, the family left Juárez on a church-sponsored visitor visa to stay in Texas for a few months. Anay's little brother, Héctor, and his young wife, Suzi, moved into their house. Héctor was working long hours in construction. Anay called me one Saturday morning. "It is awful. They raped Suzi!" She broke down crying. "She cannot even speak any more. She just stares. She won't eat. Last Thursday night, Héctor had to work late. A man broke into my house and raped her!"

I could only respond with a weak, "Oh, no!" and some questions.

"No, they are not in the house now. They moved out. She won't go back there. They are staying at my mother's house for now. Héctor cannot leave her to go to work. Poor Suzi. I can't be there to talk to her. She is so nice. Why did they do that to her?" About two weeks later, Anay reported that Suzi was eating and talking a little, but she would not go outside. The emotional trauma still overpowered her.

While Enrique and Anay lived in the house, drunks or suspicious strangers tried several times to break in. Enrique had arranged wire, blocks, and poles to make a pretty secure fence around the house. Now, however, that level of security is no protection from the escalated violence in the city. Their empty house was vulnerable, and many of their possessions were stolen while they were out of the country. When they returned from their last trip in 2009, they discovered that the neighborhood had turned into a center for drug addicts and alcoholics. Anay and Enrique abandoned the home and gave up any hope of selling it.

Just before Anay and Enrique left Juárez, Enrique had to take care of a lot of paperwork to register his car and to relocate. They stayed with me for several days, traveling back and forth to the city to work through the agencies to get the proper documents, spending many hours waiting in lines. The youngest children, Elaine and Kiké, were with them, and the two older girls stayed in Buffalo Gap, Texas, with friends from the church so that they would not miss school. On one of their day trips into Ciudad Juárez, they took the little children with them to the driver's license office to renew Enrique's license. They came back that night visibly upset as they told me the following account.

"We were sitting in the waiting room, just waiting and waiting for them to call Enrique's name so he could go and do the exam to get his new license. I saw these big black SUVs pull up. Suddenly, four men dressed in black with guns ran through this waiting room and into a back office. They came out dragging this poor girl to their trucks. She was screaming and fighting, saying, 'My name is Jennifer. It is not me! It's another girl!' We grabbed the children and covered their faces so they could not see. All the other people in the waiting room did that also, and we all looked down at the floor and did not look up. They had guns! They would kill us if we looked at them!"

The next day, I read in the Ciudad Juárez newspaper that the body of a woman was found, beheaded, on a city street. Two days later, eight more bodies of beheaded women were discovered in the city. Sadly, I suspect Jennifer was one of these women.

Two days after the incident in the license renewal office, Anay and Enrique were driving on one of the main roads in Ciudad Juárez when all of the cars in their lane of traffic had to stop behind a bus that suddenly slowed and drifted to the curb. The bus driver had just been shot and killed by the driver of an oncoming car.

In the spring of 2009, a very strong student in one of my classes suddenly quit turning in her work. She lives in El Paso, but some of her family lives in Ciudad Juárez. She called me with this account, told through her sobs: "Dr. Hampton, I am so sorry that I cannot turn in my work. I am going crazy. Please keep this information confidential. My father has been kidnapped in Juárez. He owns a business, and the kidnappers followed him around for several weeks to see who his relatives and friends are and what kind of money he might have. They are asking for a million dollars! But my family is working on getting the money. We might get him back by next week."

I was helpless to do anything other than assure her that I would make any concession necessary for her to finish the class, and offer her and her family any assistance I could. In two weeks, she called me and said that her father was safe. The family and extended family and friends had sold everything they could and had come up with half of the million dollars requested. The kidnappers accepted this and returned him—very beat up, yes, but mercifully, he was alive.

Earlier I mentioned my colleague, Alejandro Medina, who described the heavy labor required of him when he worked on industrial machines in Ciudad Juárez. Like so many people living in this part of the world, he is a resident of Mexico but also has U.S. citizenship. He earned his industrial engineering degree from the University of Texas at El Paso, but he graduated at the downturn of the economy in 2009. Like many graduates in the region at this time, he could not find work in his field in Ciudad Juárez or El Paso. He received job offers from other parts of the country but decided not to move. "I love Juárez. That is my home, and I didn't want to leave here. So, I am working on my alternative certification to be a teacher, and now I am teaching mathematics and engineering at a high school in El Paso. For all my years going to UTEP and work, I drove every day from my home in Juárez, over the bridge, every day.

"It started about three years ago, and now the city is really bad with the fight between the cartels as they struggle to see who will be the main dealers. At the beginning it did not affect my family, not in our area where we live or where we hang out. It started outside this area, but it moved rapidly to our area. I used to go out on weekends, but now they closed the bars because the cartels were demanding bribes, or quotas, as they call them. The city opened a new area that was supposed to be safe for young people to go out, but two of our friends were killed there. After that, we started to get scared. Everyone started to move here to El Paso.

"One day I was taking my cousin home from our soccer game. As I was leaving, I saw the first killing. The man had just been shot in the head. He was there in the street with blood coming out of his head. Then I was driving by Krispy Kreme and I saw a pickup with bullet holes all over it and a man inside was dead. I had to stop the car. I couldn't even drive, I was shaking so much. Another time I was coming to work in El Paso. It was about five in the morning. I crossed over a bridge in the city and there was a man hanging from the bridge. The police were just taking him down. I started to get used to [seeing the violence]. No more was I numb or having goose bumps. It started to feel normal, and it shouldn't. It should never feel normal.

"Then we started getting these phone calls with threats at my house. So we changed our phone numbers, but they still found our number and called. So we cancelled our phones, because they could get your number from some official place. I was always careful when I left the house. I looked out the curtain and looked up and down the street. One day I was at work and three guys came and tried to open our door. My mother and little brother were inside. Fortunately, we had just had those doors reinforced, so they couldn't break through. My mother called me . . . it was eleven in the morning. She was scared, but the guys left because they couldn't get in. We knew they would come back. So we hired armed guards to get her and my brother out of the house with all the clothes they could carry. We had to leave our furniture, everything over there. We got a house over here in El Paso now. We are lucky because we are citizens. They'll keep trying to get in, and if they can't get in, they'll burn the house. That's what they do. There was a motorcycle shop near our house. He did not pay their bribes and he closed the shop and moved to El Paso. So they burned it.

"They have these *halcones* [hawks]. They wait at an intersection and when a nice car or truck goes by, they write down the license plate [number]. Then they check it in the city offices and find out where you live. I saw the guy doing that at the corner. He wrote my license, and when I went back by that corner he was writing another guy's license number.

"You can't trust the police. There were some honest police, but they are in danger. Once, these police got a call that there was an emergency. They were ambushed and all killed on the way to that call. I think the other police knew they were honest. I say that if you are in trouble, call TV Channel 44. That will stop them, but not the police. There are police all over the city. But a few days ago, two trucks went shooting each other. It went on for five miles! All those police, and none on that five mile stretch? And one of the national soldiers killed the mayor's bodyguard yesterday."

The assassin-turned-Christian who was interviewed by Molloy and Bowden (2011) said that when his men needed to kill someone, they would call the head of the police department and instruct him to make sure that there were no police in the area of the killing. The police department would comply, just as Alejandro described. The informant went on to tell how his drug cartel sent him to the U.S.-sponsored police training. He became a well-trained drug assassin posing as a Ciudad Juárez police officer. He was probably using a weapon that originated in the United States. Statistics from the U.S. Bureau of Alcohol, Tobacco, Firearms and Explosives show that, of the firearms recovered by U.S. authorities in Mexico in 2009–2010, some 15,131 firearms, 70 percent, originated in the United States (Perez, 2011).

Though Alejandro is safe, he is concerned about his home-
land and family members who still live there. "Now I worry
about my aunts who are still there. It was sad the last few months
I was there. I couldn't call any friends. They all moved to El
Paso. Our neighborhood was almost empty. That is why they
came after us. Our house is pretty nice and they knew we were
still there. I love my city. I miss the good old days. My whole
family was over there. Every Sunday we would all get together at
my grandmother's house, but no more."

INTERPRETIVE CONTEXT:
CROSS-BORDER SOLIDARITY

Complex political and economic histories have led to a dichotomy between these neighboring nations—a dichotomy
most extreme in the border communities. I know that my desire for cheaper cars and vacuum cleaners, my fellow citizens'
desires for marijuana and cocaine, the flow of U.S. weapons into
Mexico, and our leaders' bungled attempts to intervene in the
Mexican economy have contributed to the damage in this broken city. Perhaps some of the U.S. policy makers who entered
the free trade agreements with Mexico were thinking of ways to
benefit that country, or at least to encounter mutual benefit. The
maquiladora industry itself is regarded by many as a benevo-
lent partnership with the Mexican border communities because
it gives jobs to people who would not have jobs otherwise. From
my viewpoint, this foreign factory phenomenon, in the context
of low wages and stress on the cities' infrastructure, is, at best,
a lateral move for Mexican citizens coming from the interior,
and at worst, a Frankenstein—one that we created—tromping
through the city and wreaking havoc. Long-term positive impact seems a vapor. We are lost in our outrageous ignorance,
trying to impose reform from our positions of power. This ignorance projects itself onto our incompetence and our inability to
cause sustained, positive change.

I ache deeply and sleep sporadically, struggling with the

question, *what can be done*? Anay is safe for now. Good people in the El Paso and Las Cruces areas support a few religious and nonprofit organizations trying to provide assistance to Mexicans seeking refuge. The researchers I have cited in this book write and publish in their effort to keep the violence in public view so that we do not turn away, yawn, and ignore the heartaches so close to our home. And some activists generate binational solidarity actions to stir the media and politicians with the knowledge that throngs of citizens are deeply concerned. I mention a few of them here.

Diana Washington Valdez, the *El Paso Times* reporter, has documented (2006) the solidarity movements that have been initiated by the mothers of the slain girls and other advocates. One of these movements was the women's march in February 2003. The Women in Black, a group of mothers and advocates, marched from Ciudad Chihuahua to Ciudad Juárez (250 miles) dressed in black dresses and pink hats. Black crosses inside of pink rectangles have become the symbol of the feminicides. As you drive on the streets in Ciudad Juárez, you will see many telephone poles painted with this symbol. The state governor at the time of the march, Patricio Martínez, ordered the police to deter or prevent the march; and, indeed, the women met resistance from the police. But they persisted, and when they arrived in Ciudad Juárez, the marching throngs swelled to thousands. The women forcefully placed a large wooden cross about ten feet tall, in the center of the auto lanes leading out of downtown Juárez over the international bridge to El Paso. The cross is adorned with spikes and personal items memorializing the slain women. It is a bold and obtrusive monument, impossible to overlook. The women defied officials to take it down, and it is still there as of 2011. (A photograph of the cross can be seen at http://frontera.nmsu.edu/main.html.)

On Valentine's Day 2004, Kathleen Staudt and others organized the "largest-ever cross-border solidarity march in this region, estimated at 5,000 to 8,000 people" (Staudt, 2008). Jane Fonda and Sally Field were among the stars leading the U.S. side of the march, and Mexican stars and dignitaries led the Mexican side. The popular feminist play *The Vagina Monologues* was performed in El Paso and Ciudad Juárez in Spanish and English. The activists met on the international bridge over the Rio Grande and continued marching through downtown Ciudad Juárez. I participated in that march, along with hundreds, maybe thousands, of marchers. We chanted, "*Ni una más! Ni una más!*" "Not one more! Not one more!" and carried signs with pink crosses. Through the crowded streets I walked along with a group of activists, young men from a fraternity at the University of Texas at El Paso, who carried signs, professionally printed, with slogans of support. We paused at the bridge as the dignitaries met and spoke, but the crowd was so vast I could not see the action. I had to watch the news that night to see the speeches that I missed. After about an hour, we started moving again and walked right through the border check lanes into downtown Ciudad Juárez, where we were able to mingle with the Mexican activists. Mothers of the slain women led our march and spoke to the crowds. When the activities began to fade, I found my way back to the U.S. border station to enter the security check lanes and return home.

As I was standing in one of these lanes to get back to El Paso, by a rare chance, I saw Enrique in this crowd of hundreds of crossers. I wiggled through the crowd and caught up to him. He greeted me with warmth and surprise. He was on his way to El Paso to borrow money from someone at the church. Anay had given birth to their third daughter early that morning. Mother and baby were fine, but the clinic charged two hundred dollars per day, and they would not release her until the bill was paid in full. We made it to the bank just before closing, and Anay and baby went home that night. It was several weeks before I was able to see them again. I picked up the little girl with those big brown eyes, and that is when Anay told me, "Her name is Elaine." I felt rippling waves of warm butter in a space behind my breast; my heart had liquefied.

Perhaps the most significant organized effort occurred in June 2011 (Llorca, 2011). Javier Sicilia, a well-known Mexican poet, known for writing about spiritual themes, vowed to write no more after his son was killed March 38, 2011, an innocent victim of the violence surrounding the drug cartels. Rather than remain passive, he organized the week-long Caravan for Peace with Justice and Dignity. About 1,500 Mexicans marched and rode buses the 1,800 miles from the poet's hometown of Cuernavaca to Ciudad Juárez and then into El Paso, where they met marchers from the U.S. side. Stages and loud speakers were set up on both sides of the border, and several individuals, rally organizers and family members of those affected by the violence, took their turns offering statements urging binational action to end the violence. When Sicilia took the stage, he called for action from the policy makers in his country that would result in responsible government and a stronger system of justice. Then he reminded the audience that the United States is the world's largest market for illegal drugs and that weapons from the United States arm the drug gangs. He recommended that the United States allow asylum to Mexicans who flee the violence. Sicilia also recommended that the United States stop funding the Mérida Initiative, which provides $1.3 billion to the Mexican Army, since this money ends up in the hands of the drug cartels. "The U.S. has a grave responsibility in all this, when its citizens remain silent, they are imposing war on us . . . . Behind every puff of pot, every line of coke, there is death, there are shattered families" (Llorca, A3).

SEVEN

Leaving Ciudad Juárez

Several weeks before Anay graduated from high school, she called with exciting news. She and Enrique had new jobs. An innovative program provided by some level of Mexican government was funding job training for citizens who were seeking work. Those selected would participate in a six-week training program where they received a very small salary along with the promise of a job upon completion of the training.

Anay was selected for training to work in a quality control capacity for new cosmetologists who were starting their careers, eventually providing on-the-job training for these new hires in the city's beauty salons. Enrique was selected to train with a chef. He was placed at one of the most elegant restaurants in Ciudad Juárez, María Chuchena's. He completed the six weeks and seemed to have enjoyed it greatly. When I visited them during this time, Enrique listed off many Mexican gourmet dishes that he could make, including the complex Mexican classic dish, *chile en nogadas*, made of a mild green *chile poblano* stuffed with several meats and raisins and covered with a rich cream sauce and pomegranate seeds. When he told me about this experience, he was animated, and I sensed a joy and pride in this career option.

"They paid me a little, but I got some good tips also. I learned so much. They told me that I was very good. I could make the complex dishes. I even created a new salsa, and the main chef said that he wanted to know how I did it. I told him he would have to pay for the recipe, but I was just joking with him."

We dream-talked together about a time when he would be a chef in a great restaurant. He did finish the training, but he lost all hope of finding a chef's job, as the competing drug gangs burned down many restaurants in the city and forced others to close. The more fortunate restaurant owners closed their restaurants in Ciudad Juárez and were able to open new ones in El Paso. María Chuchena's, for example, closed down and moved to an elegant location in El Paso. Enrique's opportunities to work as a chef vanished, and he started the painful process of finding some sort of new income source to support his family. Anay completed six weeks of her training before the family moved to Texas on a visitor's visa.

A TEMPORARY HOME IN BUFFALO GAP, TEXAS

Several members of the Church of Christ in Buffalo Gap, Texas, who were working through a church in El Paso, sponsored medical missions in the maquiladora community on the southern edge of Ciudad Juárez that Anay and Enrique called home. The doctors provided medical supplies and consultations to address basic health issues or recommend additional treatment—all free of charge to their neighbors. While waiting in line, other members from the affiliate churches in the United States visited with and sometimes evangelized these neighbors through games, skits, and translated conversations. Through these visits, the Texas church members became friends with the Carrillos.

The Buffalo Gap team, led by a soft-spoken man with a white beard named Roger Jensen (quickly adopted as "Grandpa" by the Carrillo children), visited several times and grew to love Enrique and Anay's family. About the time of Anay's high school graduation, Enrique learned that the church in El Paso would no longer be able to provide the three hundred dollars per month that it had been paying him for his work. When the Buffalo Gap church friends learned about this, and learned that Anay could not go to school for ten months after her high school graduation, especially in light of the dangerous environment in Ciudad Juárez, they petitioned the other members of their small church to sponsor the family to stay in Buffalo Gap for six months on a visitor visa. In this there would be some benefit for the church and its community as the Carrillo family could help with their Spanish-language mission work. The church members readily agreed, and they contributed sufficient funds to rent a fully furnished mobile home for the family in Buffalo Gap, to pay all their utility bills, and to provide one hundred dollars per week for spending money. The family loaded up the compact car in July 2008 and drove to Buffalo Gap. I sent Anay off with a cell phone and lots of hugs. She called me three days after they arrived.

"It is very beautiful here. We have two bathrooms and two bathtubs! One is very big. As soon as we were in the house, the girls got in the bathtub and played for hours. I have a washer and dryer, a stove, real cabinets, and, get this, running water! Yes, oh, it is so wonderful. They are so nice to us.

"One of the ladies of the church took us shopping in Abilene. We went to Dillard's, and she bought two very fancy church dresses for each of the girls and a little suit for Kiké. And she bought each of them two pairs of shoes. When I saw the price of all those clothes, I said, 'Why don't we go to Walmart or Payless? This is too much money.' She said, 'No, they need good quality.' Some days when we come home, there is a bag of toys sitting by our front door, or maybe some toilet paper, or some food, or a bag of clothes. They are so good to us.

"And, can you believe it? The girls are going to school, and they are going to pay for Enrique and me to go to school to learn English!"

I was eager to see them in this new environment, so late

in November 2008 my husband and I drove to Buffalo Gap to visit the family in their new home. Anay and Enrique spoke to us as though they were living a dream. The girls were bubbling and insisted on showing me each item of clothing in their closets and every new toy. Anay picked up a little toy stuffed lamb. When she pushed a switch, a recording in the lamb played the song, "Mary Had a Little Lamb." The girls were picking up English words very quickly. Anay grinned at me with a wink and asked her little daughter, Elaine, to sing the lamb's song for us. Elaine sang,

> Mary had a little lamb, little lamb, little lamb.
> Mary had a little lamb, *y dice Juárez, NO!*

(. . . and it says Juárez, No!) In her child's mind, the little lamb was singing a bilingual song that included "no" to a return to Ciudad Juárez.

The mobile home had a master suite on one end, a kitchen and living room in the middle, and two bedrooms and a small bath on the other end. Anay, Enrique, and the three little children slept in one of the small bedrooms, Eva in the other one. They never used the master bedroom, but slept all close together in the two small rooms on the opposite side of the house, apparently more comfortable sleeping close together as they had done in Mexico.

By this time, little Eva was speaking to us in complete English phrases. She could understand almost everything we said to her in English. Anay and Enrique were progressing rapidly, but Eva was clearly ahead. Eva showed us her certificate from school. She was the top student in her first-grade class, and the teachers quickly moved her into second grade. She and Juliet were the only Spanish speakers in the school.

Anay cooked a celebration meal for us—*gorditas*, which translates to "little fat ones." She mixed up a bowl of the corn flour dough called *masa*, formed it into palm-sized patties, and fried them until they were golden brown. When they cooled, she sliced them open lengthwise and scraped the soft dough out of the middle so we were left with a crisp shell. Into this shell she placed hamburger meat cooked with potatoes and seasoned with garlic, *chile*, and other spices. She handed us our *gorditas* and instructed us to stuff them with more items—lettuce, cheese, and tomatoes—and topped it all with a fiery hot sauce. Anay and Enrique are the master cooks; I am a novice, so my job was to wash dishes and cooking utensils. It was very pleasant to visit together while the children played with their new toys in their new living room.

"One day, Enrique and I fixed tamales for everyone in the church. They were so happy. It took a long time—two hundred tamales! But they still talk about it. We have potlucks sometimes. That is fun. But, get this! I wanted to have a real turkey for Thanksgiving dinner. Roger and Phyllis invited us to Thanksgiving dinner, but we had pork chops, not turkey. We liked them a lot, but it wasn't turkey, and we didn't have enough grocery money to buy a turkey. When we were still living in Juárez, the people from the church in El Paso gave us a big turkey for Thanksgiving. But we only had a little toaster oven. So I cut the turkey up into small pieces and gave most of it away to the neighbors so they could also cook it in their small ovens. So, in Juárez, we had the turkey and no oven. Here in Buffalo Gap, we have the oven and no turkey!" She laughed at her own joke.

We went with the family to a Sunday morning service at the small church in Buffalo Gap. There were about two hundred people, and many of them stopped me after church to tell me about their memorable experience with the Carrillo family—playing with the kids, learning how to fix tamales, learning Spanish words, and telling about how the family befriended and cared for the people who lived in their neighborhood. No one mentioned a problem communicating through the language differences.

Grandpa Roger and the other church leaders helped the family obtain a second six-month visitor visa, so they were able to stay one full year in Texas. Anay and Enrique continued serving the community and managed a small food and clothing distribution center for individuals in need. Enrique taught Bible classes in Spanish. Eva continued excelling in school. The other members of the family began conversing in broken English, and Kiké even developed a west Texas drawl when he spoke his few English phrases. The church's love of the Carrillo family grew stronger over the months. Roger told me that the Carrillos became very well known in Buffalo Gap. "If there is anyone in Buffalo Gap who needs something, they will soon find Anay or Enrique and one or two children on their doorstep with help—some fruit, an offer to babysit children, a home-cooked meal. One day I came to church and saw Enrique and Carl, a businessman who always wears a suit, crawling out from under Carl's car. Enrique had just taught Carl how to fix his car! There is this new wave of love in our church since the Carrillos came. We are reenergized!"

BACK TO MEXICO

Opportunities for a better life in Ciudad Juárez buckled and collapsed under the unstable social and economic conditions in 2009. The drug wars had escalated to a level of atrocious violence as described previously. From time to time during their year in Buffalo Gap, Anay and Enrique had to return to Ciudad Juárez for business and doctor's visits. After returning from one trip to the city, Enrique told me, "We cannot go back there. Do you know what we saw? These little girls, some twelve- and thirteen-years-old, walking around the main plaza in Ciudad Juárez asking men if they wanted to have sex. I guess the drug gangs kidnapped them. What can we do about that?" Whatever gods there may be had apparently abandoned Ciudad Juárez.

Therefore, in spite of their love for their home in northern Mexico, returning to that environment with four young children had to be discarded as a viable option. Could they some-how stay in the United States? For Mexicans, opportunities to work in the United States suffered with tighter immigration laws, stepped-up deportation, and the economic downturn in late 2008 and 2009. Despite the low odds of being permitted to extend the family's visas, the Buffalo Gap church leaders hired an immigration lawyer and searched diligently for any way to help the family stay in Texas and serve in their ministry. After several months of struggling through the tangled bureaucracy and the strict immigration policies of this era, all doors for that option slammed shut.

The church did not give up, however. Families and church leaders met together and agreed to contribute a significant amount of money (along with some contributions from out-side church members) to pay for the family to move back to Anay's home in Huixpan. With this, the church would be able to provide enough money so that the family could relocate, rent a house, and meet their economic needs. Grandpa Roger even gave them his pickup, the twelve-year-old, pristine treasure pulled from its privileged place in his garage.

When Roger called to tell me the church's decision, I re-mained quiet on the phone, waiting for the catch—maybe a set of restrictions and expectations for serving as their missionary in that part of the world—money contingent upon the church's definition of success. What Roger said instead was, "We are not putting any restrictions on the Carrillos. We don't understand the people or the culture like they do. We visited with them, and together we agreed on a vision, '. . . to share the life-giving love, joy, and hope of Jesus in relationship with the people of south-ern Mexico, as the church of Jesus Christ.' However they want to do that, we trust them."

Perhaps Anay's dream of a university education could come true. The doctor declared her cancer free, and there is a teacher preparation university nearby, just a short commute from Huix-pan. The family loaded up the truck and made the long trip south in January 2010.

INTERPRETIVE CONTEXT:
EXODUS FROM CIUDAD JUÁREZ

An Associated Press article from the *El Paso Times* (2010) provided data that seems to confirm my observations about the changing population in Ciudad Juárez. "No one knows how many residents have left the city of 1.4 million since a turf battle over border drug corridors unleashed an unprecedented wave of cartel murders and mayhem. Business leaders, citing government tax information, say the exodus could number 110,000, while a municipal group and local university say it's closer to 230,000, and estimates by social organizations are even higher."

A similar article published a few months later described the pattern of the exodus. First, the violence enters the community. Then the people search for any way to escape by relocating somewhere in Mexico or moving to El Paso. Then their abandoned house is vandalized, and eventually the neighborhood is mostly abandoned. The director of the city's Chamber of Commerce stated that about six thousand businesses have closed. The newspaper in Ciudad Juárez, *El Diario*, stated that about half of the restaurants and a fourth of the bars that were in the city three years ago are closed now because of the kidnappings, extortion, and economic crisis (*Borderland Beat*, 2011). Some predict that there eventually will be three zones in the city: the first one near the border inhabited by people with higher incomes, a zone around the edge of the city where individuals with low incomes will live, and a zone in between full of abandoned buildings.

I drove through the main streets of the city with a taxi driver in January 2011. He pointed to many maquiladoras that were closed and abandoned. Two friends who worked in different maquiladoras told me that their factories were closing. Another friend said that her factory is continually scaling back. All three report extreme security measures at their plants, such as locking down the building as soon as the shift begins. Higher-paid employees vary their routes to and from the factory each day, or they are escorted by bodyguards.

That evening in early 2011, as my taxi arrived at the center of Ciudad Juárez approaching the border, the driver said, "Look, it is eight o'clock, and we are almost the only ones on the street. It is a ghost town. They ripped the heart out of my city."

EIGHT

The Missionary and the Beauty School

Anay and her family had moved 1,500 miles away, and I did not hear from her for months. Her computer was not working. She had access to a telephone, but the technology to make calls to the United States was difficult to manipulate and very costly. I tried calling the number she gave me, but the calls did not go through. She could use an Internet café, but the owner raised rates and the costs added up quickly. Also, Anay and Enrique were extremely busy. I was uneasy about their new world and was anxious to know what was happening, so I purchased a plane ticket. I told Anay the dates of my trip during one of the few conversations we shared on the phone. She called me a few days later and told me that their cell phone had been stolen, so I should not accept any calls from that number. Then the line went dead. I e-mailed her to remind her of my arrival, but I never heard back, and the departure date was drawing near. I took a deep breath and thought back to our times together and how dependable she is and how she remembers every detail. I paid a high price for an El Paso taxi driver to take me to the airport in Ciudad Juárez, and I boarded the plane.

When I arrived at the airport, still two hours from their home, no one was there to meet me. I found a snack bar and purchased a bottle of water, read the paper, and breathed deeply over and over to try to keep my pulse rate under control. After an hour, I started visiting with the taxi drivers and the car rental agencies. I knew where Uncle Margarito's store was in Huixpan. Maybe I could drive there and someone would direct me to their home. Maybe I could manage the bus system and all the exchanges for that two-hour trip.

I turned away from the car rental booth, looked up, and saw four children with big smiles squealing and running to me with open arms. Anay was with them and Enrique was waiting outside in the truck. I grabbed Anay and hung on tight—she was alive and well, and I was not stranded.

Grandpa Roger's pickup has a large cab, so Enrique, Anay, and I were in the front and the four children were secured in their seat belts in the back. I handed little fun packs to the children—stickers, markers, small toys, and games. Eva was nine years old and spoke to me almost entirely in English. Anay's English had improved to the point that we spoke at least half of the time in English. Juliet was also able to conduct short conversations in English. Elaine and Kiké were still learning and practiced words and phrases with me. Enrique said he would stick with Spanish for now. Anay spoke to the children in English from time to time and made them watch one hour of English-language shows every day, sometimes a movie video and sometimes a television show.

We took a leisurely route from the airport to their home and drove through mountain lands where coffee grew on the family *ranchitos*—organically grown, shade-grown coffee. Enrique pointed out cement slabs in front of some of the houses. "That is where they dry the coffee beans." I enjoyed the scenery, but I was more interested in talking to the children, watching them take turns playing with the gifts, and listening to Anay tell all that they had been doing. Higher up in the mountains, Enrique turned off the highway and drove down a steep dirt road to a small valley with a stream running through it. There were two palm-topped shades and two concrete grills near the stream. A pickup was parked under the shade, and two families were cooking, visiting, and playing in the water. "*¡Hermano!*" (Brother!), they shouted when they saw Enrique walking toward them. Anay introduced me and there were hugs all around. The women were making homemade tortillas and roasted chicken on the grills. We were warmly invited to join, but Enrique told them that we had just eaten in the city. Anay and Enrique visited with the adults about church matters, and I followed the children to the stream. The cool water was very inviting on that hot day, but Anay had instructed the children specifically to avoid getting wet. So we settled for watching the other children splash and swim and tossing pebbles. As we were driving away, Anay said, "Those two men, they did not go to school, well, maybe first or second grade. See those mountains up that way? They are all part of the national wildlife reserve, a big wilderness with a jungle and monkeys way up high. Those two guys are the experts in this wilderness. Hikers from the United States and some from Europe too—right, Enrique? They come here and they hire those guys to be their guides through the wilderness. They are very smart. Maybe you can bring some other Americans, and we can all hire them and go on a big hike someday."

Enrique's mission extends to villages in these mountains, so he took this opportunity to show me the area and visit with some of his church friends. He was planning a church retreat for the people in many of the communities around Huixpan to take place the following weekend. Enrique wanted to update these church friends and assure them that he would come by Saturday morning with his pickup to gather people who needed a ride. I calculated that this had to be a three-hour trip to reach all the villages he mentioned.

From the 1930s through the 1970s, there was a strong movement of Protestant missionary efforts originating in the United States and reaching into Mexico and other countries in Latin America. Many of these efforts focused on evangelizing the indigenous populations in those countries. Through the advances of radio and television in the 1960s, along with the translation of the Bible into indigenous languages, these efforts were strengthened, resulting in many conversions to the Protestant faith. The evangelical Protestants were particularly strong, and versions of evangelical churches are still well represented in south-

ern Mexico. Over time and distance, the affiliation with the
U.S. churches weakened and unique doctrines were born from
a charismatic leader and his interpretations of religious teachings, most often rooted in strict conservative doctrines. In many
of these groups, women maintain submissive roles and are required to dress in modest long skirts and blouses in muted grays
and browns, wearing simple, if any, jewelry, long hair, and no
makeup. In general, the Protestant groups taught against ancient Catholic practices and celebrations where excesses in the
use of alcohol occurred. There is some evidence that the use of
alcohol has declined in some communities because of the Protestant teachings. Certainly, these modifications in cultural practices have multiple impacts, sometimes beneficial; but the intrusion of a new teaching into an ancient culture places additional
stress on social structures (Kahn, 2002, and Eber, 2000). Religion's intrinsic demand for an unwavering ideology contributes
to fractures in the community and fighting within families.

Some of Anay's family are evangelicals and are very opposed to the missionary work that Enrique is doing because he
encourages a less doctrinal approach. Enrique's work is not easy,
but he talked positively of his progress in the work that the Buffalo Gap Church of Christ had assigned to them. Anay supports
and assists Enrique when she can, and she describes his mission:
"These churches are still stuck in the 1960s with many supersti-
tions. There is a lot of work to do."

Toward evening, we arrived at their new home on a quiet
street on the outskirts of Huixpan, where the city melted into
agricultural fields and untamed nature. Uncle Lalo's store was
three buildings to the south of the house, and a field of corn
filled the lot to the north. Every morning, Aunt Alicia's roosters
crowed at sunrise, and shortly after that, the van-taxis, known as
colectivos, full of commuters passed by on their way into town.
This was a real house with three bedrooms, adequate storage, a
working bathroom, and running water, of a sort. In most Mexican cities there is a water delivery system, but the purification at
the source is not at the same level as in the United States, so five-
gallon water jugs of clean water are standard in most Mexican

homes. But with running water, they could wash dishes in the kitchen sink and could shower under that little stream of cold water that dribbled from the showerhead—a big advance from the bucket sponge baths in their Ciudad Juárez home. Enrique had made several pieces of attractive and sturdy cedar furniture, such as the headboard for their bed, carved with their initials—elaborate, intertwining E and A. The back porch, a concrete floor covered by a large palm-top roof, housed the washing machine, clothesline, ironing board, storage bins, and a mesh hammock dangling between the roof posts. An iguana also lived in that palm-top roof, a common food source in that part of the world. Enrique tried to catch it, but so far, the iguana had avoided the stew pot.

During our trip from the airport, Anay mentioned a young man who was living with them, Luis. She told of how she met him. "One day I was riding in the *colectivo*. I saw a young man who was very dirty counting out Mexican coins, so I knew that he was someone who had recently crossed into Mexico from a Central American country and was homeless. I said for him to come to our house for a shower and some food and that he could stay the night with us." That was several weeks ago, and he was still living with them. He had completed high school in Honduras but could not find work, so he crossed into Mexico looking for some source of income. Anay and Enrique put him to work. He helped Anay with her business by recruiting new students and working at the reception desk. He went with Enrique on his church trips to the mountains and was learning how to teach Bible classes. For breakfast one day, he taught us all how to make a fruit drink from the star-shaped fruit growing on a tree in their backyard. He picked up a broom or a cleaning rag many times a day to help keep house for a busy family of six, now eight, with Luis and me. The patio was his room, and the hammock was his bed.

The next day we visited the Instituto de Cosmetología de Huixpan, Anay's beauty school, where she teaches hair treatments, human relations, and massage. Previously, I had thought that her two years in cosmetology school in Ciudad Juárez were a wasted effort. But when she arrived in Huixpan, she searched and researched to determine the needs of the community. Clearly, women's education was a need. She noticed that there were very few beauty salons or barber shops serving the town, and certainly none in the rural villages. She had the certificate and the experience to open a school to train cosmetologists, so she met with the state education department (Secretaría de Educación Pública) and began the paperwork to start this effort.

The school was located in a strip of stores in a long building along one of the main streets in Huixpan. It's the one painted Anay's favorite color, bright lime green. The man who owned the building was very generous in allowing Anay to rent the space on a pay scale that slides with her student enrollment. Enrique built a new reception desk and a wall to separate the classroom space from the laboratory space. He put up shelves and repaired twenty used student desks they had found on sale. Anay helped paint the rooms and purchased the equipment for the laboratory, government-required postings for her license, exit signs, and safety signs. She hung Grandpa Roger's picture by the reception desk. Her students were required to purchase their uniform shirt—a lime-green collared tee shirt with the Instituto's name embroidered over the left pocket in bright pink.

At the time of my visit, Anay was conducting three sessions with a total of forty students enrolled, one man and the rest women. One session was held on Monday, Wednesday, and Thursday mornings to accommodate the schedules of the students who had children in elementary school; the late afternoon session, also three times a week, was set up to accommodate students who were working all day or attending another school; and the third session met all day on Saturdays for those students who could not attend during the week. The students paid by the month. Each semester was four months long, and a student could complete the entire course and achieve a state-approved certificate in eighteen months. The school had been functioning for four months.

Anay kept the building open in the middle of the day when school was not in session. Loud music was piped through an amplifier and pointed toward the street to attract attention. There was a small refrigerator with a sign advertising bottles of cold water for about eighty cents. A variety of bags of cookies and chips were also for sale, providing a little additional income to the business. The bright green shop is very noticeable, and several students have been recruited from individuals who just happened upon the school.

One day a young woman walked into the reception area. "She was dressed in this very short skirt and a blouse showing everything. I thought she was probably a prostitute. But she wanted to go to school here. She did not have any money. I couldn't stay at the school all the time, and I needed a receptionist. So, after we talked a long time, I told her that we could give her a job for a day or two to try out how she would do as a receptionist. I gave her one of the green shirts and told her to go in the office and put it on. She came out crying and crying. She said that is the only time that anyone had given her some nice clothes and treated her with respect. She has been alone for a long time since they kicked her out of her house, and she had to go with men to get some money and food. But she stayed working for me for several weeks. Then she got the phone number for her uncle who lives nearby in [the big city] and called him. He said she could come live with him if she wanted to go to high school. So that is where she is now. She wants to get her education. I liked her a lot. I hope she is doing well now."

Now Anay employs four people, providing them a small but acceptable income. So far Anay has no salary, but she showed me the math in her accounting plan and it appeared to me that she should have a small income soon. Luis does the recruiting and home visits to help the women register and do the government paperwork. One young man works at the reception desk all morning, and a young woman works all afternoon.

Mónica (all the women's names are pseudonyms), who signed up to be a student, had had some training in cosmetology, but no certification. She was able to teach for Anay from time to time, and she assisted in some of the bigger classes in return for reduced tuition. Mónica came to Anay from a violent domestic situation with a husband who abused her. She told Anay that she had been pregnant, but he hit her so hard she lost the baby. "I was going to beauty school when I lived with him. But I had to stop because if I asked him for money to pay for school, he hit me. If I didn't ask, he didn't hit me. So I left him, but my parents would not help me. I moved in with my brother. He is nice to me, but he cannot help me pay for anything." The job with Anay offers her this opportunity to finish cosmetology school, and, in exchange, Anay has some assistance in the growing business.

Anay had planned an informal lunch for the women in the morning session and invited me to join them. The students gathered in the classroom, Anay provided a few updates, and then she introduced me and told them that I was going to describe the school to friends in the United States. So the women openly shared with me information about their schooling experiences. Margarita, a single mother with three children in high school, is planning to use her training to help provide income for the children's continuing education. Angélica's husband is a mechanic with a good income; but with their four children plus the two relatives' children they adopted, costs for education are more than she can pay. She said that the local schools charge about US$6.40 per child per month. She hopes to open her own beauty salon and work in her home. Lupe told me, "*La vida es dura*" (life is hard) and went on to say that although her husband is a hard worker, he does not have enough income to buy the necessities for her and her one child. No one in her community, thirty minutes away, cuts hair, so she is hopeful that she can gain income with her training. Lucía travels almost two hours to arrive at the school and muttered thanks to God that her mother helps her pay for the schooling. Teresa has two children in elementary school, and although her husband helps her pay the schooling fees, there is not enough money to buy any equipment to start her own shop. Rosa is the oldest of three sisters whose parents work in the United States. An aunt lets the girls live in her home. One of the adult sisters has serious developmental problems and has to wear diapers and be fed blended foods. Rosa makes very good grades and wants this career so she can provide for her sisters and, hopefully, pay for advanced education. I was able to visit only a short time with some of the students in the afternoon session. At least six of the thirteen students were also seeking a career, but a few of these students were high school girls who just wanted to know how to fix hair and do beauty treatments. The women all called Anay "Profe."

Most of the women stated that paying for their cosmetology schooling was difficult, but they were managing. However, paying for all the equipment they would need to start their own careers might be a barrier that they cannot overcome. In order to purchase this equipment—electric razor, comb and scissor sets, permanent wave rollers, capes, curling irons, manicure sets—they have to travel to a large city about two hours away, and there the equipment is very expensive. So Anay will start a small microloan program for the women who graduate. With a little help from U.S. friends, she will purchase several sets of the needed equipment. A woman can take a set with her and pay Anay back in very small payments over extended time. "We can start with this. I think they will be honest and pay me back. If not, I'll take the equipment back. If this works, maybe we can help women purchase something else that they need, like maybe a cow or a sewing machine. But we'll start with this plan first."

Meanwhile, Anay is continuing her own educational goals. She found a school of higher education with a flexible schedule that would squeeze into her overflowing commitments. She gets up very early every Sunday morning and drives about an hour and a half to a nearby town to attend the university for six hours. Then she drives home to help Enrique with all his Sunday church activities. All of this while she takes online classes.

I cannot comment on the quality of the curriculum that Anay has experienced in the past or that she is now experiencing in the variety of schools that have accommodated her alternative schedules. From my interactions with her, Anay seems competent in the Spanish literacy and mathematics skills that she needs to manage her home and business accounts. Somewhere in her past, she learned how to learn—how to research, to solve problems, to overcome obstacles, and to speak a second language.

I had many happy hours talking with Anay and Enrique about their experiences and their dreams and playing with the children, reading books, having books read to me, and dining on wonderful traditional dishes. I took over my old chores at the house—washing dishes and putting them away. Anay said, *"Elaine, mi casa es tu casa; pero la cocina es mía!"* [My house is your house (the common Spanish saying of welcome); but the kitchen is mine! (implying that I was to stay out of her way)]. I watched in wonder as she chatted with me, managed the children, and, with casual ease, whipped out full meals from raw ingredients for eight people. One morning we had sweet tamales, which she made by cutting the kernels off of the corn cob, blending them with magical ingredients, stuffing this dough into corn husks, and steaming them to perfection.

One afternoon we loaded into the pickup and drove to the *ranchito* to see Eva, Francisco, and Anay's aunt and cousins. It was planned as a short visit, but before long Francisco stalked and clubbed one of the chickens, Aunt Rosie plucked it and put it in the pot, and Eva started making tortillas on the stone grill. Grandmother Eva thought it was time that I learned how to cook tortillas. Hers were all perfect circles; mine was the shape of a tree; and for the rest of the evening, that poor tortilla became the butt of many jokes. We chatted with the family and neighbors and enjoyed our feast from nature. Three boys from the neighborhood stopped by to visit, dragging two iguanas held captive in a bucket. Grandfather Francisco purchased those iguanas for tomorrow's stew.

On the way home from the *ranchito*, Anay said, "Elaine, do you know what my greatest fear is? That my children will stay here and live on a *ranchito*. I am afraid because those floods are so awful. And they do not have good education in the schools in Huixpan. The teachers are not very good. One day Eva was crying after school and could not sleep that night because the teacher had been so mean to one of her friends. We have to move soon so they can be in a place where there is good education . . . or maybe Enrique and I will start a school. You know, we talk about that. We want to have a big building. We can have sports for the kids in the town. One room will be a beauty school. Another room, maybe teach auto mechanics. Another room to teach reading and writing. And on the weekends, it can be the church. Remember that empty lot by my beauty school? We think that will be a good place. Enrique, how much did the man say he would sell it for? Well, we need to ask him again."

Dream-talking again. But so far, Anay's dreams have formed pathways that have allowed her to negotiate the complex existence for women and their families in this tropical corner of Mexico.

INTERPRETIVE CONTEXT: POSTCOLONIAL FEMINIST AGENCY

When Anay was working at the maquiladora and staying late to attend school, the man with the mask and yellow eyes tried, two times, to grab her and take her to some place too painful to imagine. But she survived both attempts. The first time, her sheer strength and determination kept her hanging onto the light pole until yellow eyes gave up. The second time, she survived because some friend came to her aid and saved her life. Her survival of the two attacks forms a metaphoric framework to help explain the agency (Bandura, 1982) of this woman of Juárez as she pursued her education through labor and violence.

First, that same strength and determination that kept Anay hanging onto the light pole was her personal agency, her self-efficacy, her human motivation and the reason she survived. And, second, that friendship with the man in the convenience store exemplified her interactive agency; he was there with assistance when she needed him. The strength she drew from her husband and children, along with her cross-cultural friendship with me, the Buffalo Gap church, and other friends from other U.S. churches, was her social capital, which contributed to her interactive agency, her moral and financial support, her social motivation, and the second source for survival. She overcame again and again—the exploitation in the factory environment, the violence that engulfed her, and the social and family events that repeatedly eliminated her educational options and forced her to dig deeper in her struggle for formal education. Her success in overcoming these odds, these barriers, "gave light to" (birthed) a second generation of interactive agency—a school full of women in southern Mexico who now have an educational choice designed by a woman who lives in this space of wispy options, designed to meet the needs of women who live there with her; a school scheduled around the demands of caring for families so that these students can achieve their education and plan for a future with a practical and dependable income stream.

Anay led me through her world, this postcolonial feminist space—a dangerous place where women, often voiceless, are left to pick through the societal debris cast off from colonizers, neoliberal economic practices, and Western political intrusions into their lives. She overcame and was able to flourish in that shadow land where so many women in developing countries dwell.

Epilogue

I n December of 2011, the first class of thirty-two students graduated from Anay's beauty school in Huixpan. In January the new cohorts began, and all sessions were full. I visited her in March, and she showed me three new beauty shops in Huixpan—evidence of her graduates' first economic adventures. In addition, she had acquired a building and equipment to open her second beauty school in a small city nearby.

Enrique was enthusiastic as he told me about his church activities involving youth rallies, medical campaigns, and preaching in small communities throughout the area. Anay was his partner in most of these activities, while keeping the active family organized, teaching classes at the beauty school, and managing and expanding her successful business.

In February of 2012, Anay, Enrique, and the children traveled to Ciudad Juárez to petition the U.S. consulate to renew their visas. The agents at the consulate had told them that they had to renew their visas in the same location where they initially received the visas. This meant two very expensive trips and the preparation of a folder full of paperwork to prove that they were living and working in Mexico and were not going to emigrate to the United States. Anay and Enrique felt that the visas were very important in order for them to visit their sponsoring churches and organize Enrique's missionary efforts.

After hours waiting in line at the consulate, they finally had an audience with an agent. He was brisk and refused to look at all their paperwork—that thick folder of information with proof of Enrique's work, Anay's business, and their roots in Huixpan. He glanced at the family, said, "Denied!" and told them to move along. Later, when I met them in Ciudad Juárez, a very disappointed Enrique showed me the denial form with the words something like this, "Decision to refuse the visa is firm. This petition cannot be contested for one year."

While they were in Ciudad Juárez for those few days, they visited with Anay's family. Her brother, Héctor, the one who helped care for the children when Anay and I took our first trip to Chiapas, told her that he was in serious trouble. For some reason, the drug gangs were after him and threatening his life and his family's safety. Anay, the Buffalo Gap church friends, and I searched for any hope for a way for Héctor to escape the gangs.

Eight days later I received a text message from her that Héctor had been killed. I sent her a message begging her to not go to Ciudad Juárez for the funeral. I was too worried about her safety. She ignored me, and three days later she sent me this text message: "I'm in Juárez with my brothers. Could I borrow $1000, and could you send it by Western Union as soon as possible . . . in a few minutes?"

I was angry and scared. What kind of trouble was she in? Why was she there? But clearly she needed help, so I sent the money. (When the people in Buffalo Gap heard about it, they sent me a check for one thousand dollars.) That evening she sent a text saying, "We are in Mexico City. I will call you when I can." When I saw her in March, she told me the whole story.

"Héctor and Suzi have two little boys. A few months ago, the oldest child was very sick with pneumonia and was in the hospital for one week. My brother had to pay the bill for the medicine and the hospital. [In most hospitals in Ciudad Juárez, the hospital administrators will not release the patient until the bill is paid.] A man lent him the money—about four hundred dollars. When it was time to pay the money back, my brother did not have the money. He looked for ways to get the money, but there was no work, and no one would help him. The man told him, 'Okay. I have a job for you.'

"And this job was to sell marijuana. Héctor had no choice, so he took the offer and worked like this for two weeks. Then he told the man, 'Okay, I paid the money. I will stop.' The man told him, 'It's too late, you can't stop. Now you need to kill someone.' My brother refused to do this.

"This was when Enrique and I were in Juárez trying to get our visas. I saw my brother. He told me what was happening. I told him to leave Juárez. He said that it is too late. If he left, they would kill his family. He hugged me and told me that he knew he would be killed. He said for me to take care of all his family—his brothers and sister, his wife, and the babies. It was very hard for me to leave. Eight days later he was shot and killed in a gang fight with the police . . . well, probably the gang members *in* the police. They had set it up for him to be killed. There were twenty-five bullets in his body."

She was sobbing as she finished the story. "I had to come to the funeral. When I got to Juárez, I went to his house and I rubbed my hand over where he had slept, and talked to him and told him that his family would be okay. I did not want to see his body; I just wanted to remember his smile.

"The next day we looked for someone who would give the sermon at the funeral. We visited four Catholic churches in Juárez, and the priests didn't want to give the sermon because they said he was not an honest man. We asked six preachers from Christian churches. They also said they did not want to give the sermon because my brother was not holy. Finally, I talked to a friend, and I explained the story of Job in the Bible, that God told the devil to touch his body, not his soul. I explained that my brother was baptized as a Christian. I explained that he was in this situation and was very repentant, but that he had no other options. I told the man, 'You have to come. I will pay your gasoline.'

"Finally this friend said, 'Don't worry. I'll give the sermon.'

"So, we all went to the funeral and the burial. After this, I talked to my brothers and told them, 'Your lives are in danger. I feel in my heart that you have to leave Juárez.' One brother said that ten days earlier Héctor had been begging them to run away from Juárez. I was afraid to go to the house, so I took them all to a hotel and talked more about leaving. I asked God for a plan on how to get them all out in different buses to different places. The wives of my oldest brothers went to their parents' houses. My brothers and my sister couldn't go back to their houses, so they all left Juárez with nothing more than the clothes on their backs.

"Four hours after we were all on the road in different directions, the gangs came to my two brothers' houses and went through all their stuff, throwing things and looking for them. If they had been there, they would have killed them.

"They have different last names, and they come from a different state. They all went in different routes to get here. So I think they cannot be followed. Now, living in my house with me, Enrique, and the children are three brothers, my sister, and my stepfather. My two oldest brothers work on the construction of the new church, work in my uncle's store a little bit, and help around the school. We have a schedule. One brother fixes breakfast. Every morning, he knocks on my bedroom door and brings coffee to me and Enrique. One brother cleans the yard and cleans the floors. My little brother and sister are in school. My sister has top grades in school and is doing very well here. They all go to the church activities with us and help with the medical campaigns and the youth rallies. They help take care of my children, so it is working well.

"We are still worried about the wives and children back in Juárez. My brother's wife is living with some family members, but it is hard for her. I am very worried about their future. I am thinking of ways that we can help all of them and help them get back home.

"But here is my motto: *Si esfuerza, pasará barreras y no habrá fronteras.*"

The rhyme and rhythm that the Spanish provides are lost in the translation, but her motto goes something like this: "If you strive hard, you will overcome barriers and there will be no borders." And I'm sure Anay will.

Notes

INTRODUCTION

1. Anay is a Mayan name, pronounced, roughly, as "an eye."

2. The city is commonly called Juárez, honoring the beloved mid-nineteenth-century Mexican president Benito Juárez. In May 2011, lawmakers in the Chihuahua state capital officially changed its name to "Heroica Ciudad Juárez," which means "Heroic Juárez City." As soon as the change was announced, a flood of comments hit the media. The state lawmakers' intent was to honor the city's important role in the 1910 Mexican Revolution; however, to those who anguish over the city's current troubles, the name change seemed out of line with the prevailing conditions of violence and despair. I use the name Ciudad Juárez in this book—the official title before the May 2011 name change.

3. The ethnographer's role is to enter a different culture and generate an ethnographic report to enlarge cultural understanding. But the researcher becomes ethically involved in the study, thus actively seeking reform and taking action during the course of the study, becoming a critically engaged activist researcher (Speed, 2006). I became a participant in the study as I became a part of Anay's life. I, along with other friends in the United States, assisted Anay and her family with emotional and financial resources, thus positioning Anay and her family in a very different situation at the time of this writing from where they would be if we had never met. I believed that I had to intervene. It would have been impossible for me to be an objective observer in Ciudad Juárez, drive home to my luxury, and forget about what Anay was going through. As you will read in the chapters that follow, Anay's economic needs are still vast as she

continues her struggle for higher education for herself and her children, and she continues to struggle against recurring cancer. Proceeds of this book will go mostly toward Anay's education and the education of women in southern Mexico.

4. Neoliberal is a term commonly used for an open market approach to trade, that is, liberalized trading practices.

5. Public Citizen's 2004 report, "The Ten-Year Track Record of NAFTA," further documents the consequences of liberalizing great swaths of Mexican economic structures. Prior to NAFTA, there were about eight million Mexicans working in agriculture, mostly through a system of small plots, called *ejidos*, permanently deeded to small rural farmers. This small farming system, implemented in 1917, ensured stable prices and provided government loans and subsidies. The main crop was corn—a major component of Mexico's agricultural and cultural identity. By joining NAFTA, the Mexican government agreed to move this agricultural system, along with many other programs, to private and sometimes foreign corporations. Some 1.5 million peasants lost their farms. "U.S. corn exports to Mexico have more than quadrupled since 1993, and have been sold at prices below what it costs U.S. farmers to grow it, causing a 70% drop in the real prices paid to Mexican farmers for their corn under NAFTA" (p. 2). Mexico no longer grows most of its own corn, instead depending on imported corn from the United States. The price of the Mexican food staple, corn tortillas, has increased by more than 50 percent since NAFTA (Public Citizen, 2004, p. 2).

6. Rafael Rodríguez Castañeda's 2009 book, *El México Narco*, is a collection of articles from reporters with the Mexican magazine *Proceso*, of which Rodríguez Castañeda is editor. These reporters provide a narco map through the Mexican states with rich details of which cartel is where at what time and for what reasons. The reporters document the names of the main players in the narco business along with events that lead to their power positions and their falls. Rodríguez Castañeda confirms that the political actions previously listed are causes of the escalation of the violence but adds his belief that these actions were catalysts to a natural progression in growth of the drug industry. The large cartels outgrew their stability and broke into smaller families, roaming and slaughtering to try to claim dominance and the wealth that accompanied it.

7. Unless otherwise stated, money amounts are given as the approximate equivalent at the time of writing.

8. Perhaps the most valuable current resources for ongoing, grassroots information about the maquiladora industry in Ciudad Juárez are

two electronic networks from New Mexico State University. Kent Patterson is the editor of the online newsletter out of the university's *Frontera NorteSur*. He and university librarian Molly Molloy, through her Google group called Frontera List, synthesize and distribute ongoing information about the maquiladora industry, border politics, border violence, and actions by activists and concerned citizens to help alleviate the problems. *Frontera NorteSur*'s website (www.nmsu.edu/~frontera) shows a picture of the large pink and black cross that rests in front of the downtown border crossing on the Mexican side.

Mujeres, Migración, y Maquila en la Frontera Norte (*Women, Migration, and Maquiladoras in the Northern Border*) is a 1995 collection of essays about women who migrate from the south of Mexico to work in the factories, some in bus or van rides like Anay's. Four essays provide insight into the industry in the context of changes in employment related to gender, in employee turnover, and in women's place in the social and familial structures of these factory environments. The editors are Soledad González Montes, Olivia Ruiz, Laura Velasco, and Ofelia Woo of the Colegio de la Frontera Norte.

CHAPTER 2

1. I am not her mother, but she gave me this title of "Mommy." In her culture, an older woman who is special in your life may be referred to as a mother, such as, "*Mi madre, Ana.*" Our relationship has now grown so that she calls me by my first name. We consider ourselves partners in this book project and in our efforts to improve education for women in southern Mexico.

2. Everyone living on the North or South American continent is considered American. The official Mexican way to refer to someone from the United States is *estadounidense*. That is a mouthful, and I often hear them refer to me as the *americana*.

3. In the heart of Mexico City, at Tlatelolco, is the Plaza of the Three Cultures. It is a very significant historic site where an Aztec temple and the first Spanish school sit in the shadow of high-rise modern Mexican government buildings. On a plaque in the plaza is a statement in Spanish that I have translated as, "On this spot on August 13, 1521, the Aztec force, heroically defended by Cuauhtémoc, fell to the power of Hernán Cortés and the Spanish army. It was neither a defeat nor a victory, but rather the painful birth of the mestizo people who are Mexico."

Alan Riding, in his Mexican history, *Distant Neighbors*, describes the mestizo:

> Today, in strictly ethnic terms, 90 percent of Mexicans are mestizos, but as individuals they remain trapped by the contradictions of their own parentage. They are the sons of both Cortés and Cuauhtémoc, yet they are neither Spanish nor Indian. They are mestizos, but they cannot accept their *mestizaje*. As a nation, too, Mexico searches endlessly for an identity, hovering ambivalently between ancient and modern, traditional and fashionable, Indian and Spanish, Oriental and Western. And it is in both the clash and the fusion of these roots that the complexity of Mexico resides (p. 4).

CHAPTER 3

1. From my conversations I gathered that in this part of Mexico most teachers are called *Profe*, short for *profesor/a*. In Ciudad Juárez, I have heard people address male teachers and high school teachers as *Profe*. Women and elementary teachers are more often called *maestra*. I felt respected when he addressed me as *Profe*.

2. More information about these schools may be found on the website schoolsforchiapas.org.

CHAPTER 4

1. Ancient traditions honoring the afterlife came from the early indigenous peoples of Mexico and were later modified to accommodate Catholic traditions. Today, Mexicans honor the dead and glorify the resurrection of loved ones through ceremonies that center around the Día de los Muertos, or Day of the Dead, on the first and second days in November. Around our Halloween, we can see traces of these colorful celebrations moving into the United States with Mexican immigrants. Elegantly dressed ceramic skeleton women called *catrinas*, candy skulls, colorful altars to dead family and friends, and community events at the cemeteries fill the season. Brightly colored flowers are very important for these events, and southern Mexico is a center for these celebrations. Ofelia grew the golden chrysanthemums that are most often used to decorate altars.

CHAPTER 5

1. I express my appreciation to the following UTEP graduate students for assistance with the student interviews and for their permission to publish those interviews: Erin Brown, Sarah Johnston, Minerva Nijera, and Ricardo Ponce.

Works Cited

Amnesty International. 2004. *It's in Our Hands: Stop Violence against Women*. London: Author.

Arizpe, Lourdes. 1997. "Women in the Informal Sector: The Case of Mexico City." *Signs* 3(1): 25–37.

Arriola, Elvia Rosales. 2001. "Looking out from a Cardboard Box: Workers, their Families and the Maquiladora Industry in Ciudad Acuña, Coahuila." *Frontera NorteSur* [electronic journal]. Retrieved May 2012 from http://www.cfomaquiladoras.org/lookingoutfrom.en.html.

Associated Press. 2011. "Countless Juárez Residents Flee Dying City." *El Paso Times*, Jan. 21. Retrieved on January 22 from http://elpasotimes.type pad.com/mexico/2011/01/exodus-from-ju%C3%A1rez-will-continue -researchers-warn.html.

Bandura, Albert. 1982. Self-Efficacy Mechanism in Human Agency. *American Psychologist* 27(2):122–137.

Becera-Acosta, Juan Pablo. 2010. "Huyeron de Juárez 500 mil Ciudadanos por la violencia." *Milienio*, Feb. 16. Retrieved June 2010 from http:// impreso.milenio.com/node/8720630.

Borderland Beat. 2011. "Business Owners Look for a Way out of Violent Ciudad Juárez." Retrieved March 5, 2011, from http://www.borderland beat.com/2011/03/business-owners-look-for-way-out-of.html

Bowden, Charles. 2010. *Murder City: Ciudad Juárez and the Global Economy's New Killing Fields*. New York: Nation Books.

Brown, Stephen Gilbert, and Sidney Dobrin, eds. 2004. *Ethnography Unbound: From Theory Shock to Critical Praxis*. Albany: State University of New York Press.

Cardona, Julián. 2012. "Juárez, Todavía la más violenta del mundo." *Juarez-Dialoga*, Feb. 6. Retreived April 2012 from http://juarezdialoga.org/ls-articulistas/juarez-todavia-la-mas-violenta-del-mundo/.

Castañeda, Jorge. 2010. "Mexico's Failed Drug War." Cato Institute Economic Development Bulletin 13 (May 6). Retrieved Jan. 15, 2010, from www.cato.org/pubs/edb/edb13.pdf.

Del Castillo, Adelaida. 1977. "Malintzin Tenépal: A Preliminary Look into a New Perspective." In *Essays on la Mujer*, edited by Rosaura Sánchez and Rosa Martínez Cruz, 141–150. Los Angeles: Chicano Studies Center, University of California.

———. 1980. "Mexican Women in Organization." In *Mexican Women in the United States: Struggles Past and Present*, edited by Magdalena Mora and Adelaida Del Castillo, 7–16. Los Angeles: Chicano Studies Research Center, University of California.

Eber, Christine. 2000. *Women and Alcohol in a Highland Maya Town: Water of Hope, Water of Sorrow* (2nd ed.). Austin: University of Texas Press.

Eber, Christine, and Christine Kovic. 2003. *Women of Chiapas: Making History in Times of Struggle and Hope*. New York: Routledge.

Estrada, Antonio. 2001. "Mexico." In *Child Abuse: A Global View*, edited by B. Schwartz-Kennedy, M. McCauley, and M. A. Epstein, 145–160. Westport, CT: Greenwood Press.

Fernández-Kelly, María Patricia. 1983. *For We Are Sold, I and My People: Women and Industry in Mexico's Frontier*. Albany: State University of New York Press.

Flores-Ortiz, Yvette G. 1999. "Theorizing Justice in Chicano Families." JSRI Occasional Paper #43. East Lansing, MI: The Julián Samora Research Institute, Michigan State University.

Flores Simental, Raúl, Efrén Gutiérrez Roa, and Oscar Vázquez Reyes. 1998. *Crónica en el Desierto: Ciudad Juárez de 1659 a 1970*. Ciudad Juárez, Chihuahua, México: Junta Municipal de Agua y Saneamiento de Juárez.

Floyd, Chris. 2010. "Manufacturing Mayhem in Mexico: From Nixon to NAFTA and Beyond." Frontera-list, Oct. 28. Available at http://chris-floyd.com/articles/1-latest-news/2039-manufacturig-mayhem-in-mexico-from-nixon-to-nafta-and-beyond.html.

Franco, Pilar. 1999. "Informal Sector: A Billion Dollar Lifebelt." InterPress Third World News Agency. Retrieved November 20, 2010 from http://www.converge.org.nz/lac/articles/news990523a.htm.

Fregoso, Rosa-Linda, and Cynthia Bejarano, eds. 2010. *Terrorizing Women: Feminicide in the Américas.* Durham, NC: Duke University Press.

Freire, Paolo. 1996. *Pedagogy of the Oppressed* (Revised 20th Anniversary Edition). New York: Continuum International.

Frontera NorteSur. 2009 (Oct. 26). "Do Border Plants Herald Economic Recovery?" Available at www.nmsu.edu/~frontera/.

——— 2010 (Dec. 13). "Pirated Black Market Goods are Mexico's Top Money Maker." Retrieved Dec. 2010 from http://mexidata.info/id2894 .html.

Geertz, Clifford. 1988. *Works and Lives: The Anthropologist as Author.* Palo Alto, CA: Stanford University Press.

González Boz, Aureliano. 1993. "Manufacturing in Mexico: The Mexican In-Bond (Maquila) Program. The Most Commonly Asked Questions." Retrieved June 6, 2010, from http://www.udel.edu/leipzig.texts2/vox128 .htm.

Green, Jay P., and Marcus A. Winters. 2005. "Public High School Graduation and College Readiness Rates: 1991–2002." Education Working Paper, No. 8. Manhattan Institute for Policy Research. Retrieved June 6, 2010, from http://www.manhattan-institute.org/html/ewp_08.htm.

Hampton, Elaine. 2004. "Globalization Legacy: A View of U.S. Factory Involvement in Mexican Education." *Multicultural Education* 11(4):2–11.

Hart, John M. 1980. "Working-class Women in Nineteenth-Century Mexico." In *Mexican Women in the United States: Struggles Past and Present*, edited by Magdalena Mora and Adelaida Del Castillo, 151–157. Los Angeles: Chicano Studies Research Center, University of California.

Herrera Robles, Luis Alfonso. 2007. *El Desgobierno de la Ciudad y la Política de Abandono: Miradas desde la Frontera Norte de México.* Ciudad Juárez: Universidad Autónoma de Ciudad Juárez.

Iglesias Prieto, Norma. 1997. *Beautiful Flowers of the Maquiladora.* Austin: University of Texas Press.

Kahn, Ronnie. 2002. "Teaching about Religion in Latin America." Center for Caribbean and Latin American Studies. Retrieved on January 22, 2011 from http://www.clacs.illinois.edu/outreach/teachingresources /teaching/religion/default.aspx.

Kopinak, Katheryn. 1996. *Desert Capitalism: Maquiladoras in North American's Western Industrial Corridor.* Tucson: University of Arizona Press.

Llorca, Juan Carlos. 2011. "Mexican Poet Calls for Peace." *Albuquerque Journal*, June 12, A3.

Martínez, Elizabeth, and Ed McCaughan. 1990. "Chicanas and Mexicans within a Transnational Working Class." In *Between Borders: Essays on Mexicana/Chicana History*, edited by Adelaida Del Castillo, 31–60. Encino, CA: Floricanto Press.

McClusky, Laura. 2001. *Here Our Culture Is Hard: Stories of Domestic Violence from a Mayan Community in Belize*. Austin: University of Texas Press.

McNeil, Linda M. 2000. *Contradictions of School Reform: Educational Costs of Standardized Testing*. New York: Routledge.

Molloy, Molly. Frontera List. Available at http://groups.google.com/group/frontera-list.

Molloy, Molly, and Charles Bowden, eds. 2011. *El Sicario: The Autobiography of a Mexican Assassin*. New York: Nation Books.

Olivera, Mercedes. 2010. "Violencia Feminicida: Violence against Women and Mexico's Structural Crisis." In *Terrorizing Women: Feminicide in the Americas*, edited by Rosa-Linda Fregoso and Cynthia Bejarano, 49–58. Durham, NC: Duke University Press.

O'Reilly, Karen. 2009. *Key Concepts in Ethnography*. Thousand Oaks, CA: Sage Publications.

Padgett, Tim. 2011. Day of the Dead. *Time*, July 11, 24–31.

Paz, Octavio. 1961. *The Labyrinth of Solitude*. New York: Grove Press.

Peña, Devon. (1997). *Terror of the Machine: Work, Gender, and Ecology on the U.S. Mexico Border*. Austin: University of Texas Press.

Peña, Sergio, and César M. Fuentes. 2007. "Land Use Changes in Ciudad Juárez, Chihuahua: A Systems Dynamic Model." *Estudios Fronterizos* 8(16):65–89. Retrieved May 2011 from http://redalyc.uaemex.mx/pdf/530/53081603.pdf.

Perez, Evan. 2011. "Mexican Guns Tied to U.S.: American-Sourced Weapons Account for 70% of Seized Firearms in Mexico." *Wall Street Journal*, June 10, p. A3.

Public Citizen. 2004. "The Ten-Year Track Record of the North American Free Trade Agreement: The Mexican Economy, Agriculture and Environment." Retrieved June 2010 from www.citizen.org/documents/NAFTA_10_mexico.pdf.

Rodríguez, Teresa, and Diana Montané. 2007. *The Daughters of Juárez: A True Story of Serial Murders South of the Border*. New York: Atria Books.

Rodríguez Castañeda, Rafael. 2009. *El México Narco*. Mexico City: Editorial Planeta.

Salzinger, Leslie. 2003. *Genders in Production: Making Workers in Mexico's Global Factories.* Berkeley: University of California Press.

Schutte, Ofelia. 2000. "Cultural Alterity: Cross-cultural Communication and Feminist Theory in North-South Contexts. In *Women of Color and Philosophy: A Critical Reader,* edited by Naomi Zack, 44–68. Malden, MA: Blackwell Publisher.

Seelke, Claire Ribando. 2010. Congressional Research Service Report, "Mérida Initiative for Mexico and Central America: Funding and Policy Issues." Retrieved May 2011 from http://fpc.state.gov.documents/organization/141560.pdf.

Speed, Shannon. 2006. "At the Crossroads of Human Rights and Anthropology: Toward a Critically Engaged Activist Research." *American Anthropologist* 108(1):66–76.

Staudt, Kathleen. 2008. *Violence and Activism at the Border: Gender, Fear, and Everyday Life in Ciudad Juárez.* Austin: University of Texas Press.

TeamNAFTA. 2011. "Labor and Wage Rate Trends Impacting Mexico's Maquiladoras in 2011." Retrieved April 2012 from http://www.teamnafta.com/index.php/Latest/2011-Labor-and-Wage-Report-for-Mexico.html.

Tiano, Susan. 1994. *Patriarchy on the Line: Labor, Gender, and Ideology in the Mexican Maquila Industry.* Philadelphia: Temple University Press.

U.S. Department of State. 2009. "Human Rights Report: Mexico 2009." Retrieved November 20, 2010 from http://www.state.gov/g/drl/rls/hrrpt/2009/wha/136119.htm.

Valenzuela, Angela, ed. 2004. *Leaving Children Behind: Why Texas-Style Accountability Fails Latino Youth.* Albany: State University of New York Press.

Villar, Ernesto de la Torre. 1529. *Frey Pedro de Gante: Maestro y civilizador de América.* Retrieved June 2009 from www.ejournal.unam.mx/historia_novo/ehno5/EHNO0502.pdf.

Washington Valdez, Diana. 2006. *Harvest of Women: Safari in Mexico.* Burbank, CA: Peace at the Border.

Weatherford, Jack. 1988. *Indian Givers: How the Indians of the Americas Transformed the World.* New York: Fawcett Columbine.

Index

beauty school: attending, 90–91; government program, 130; graduates of, 151; students in, 145–146. See also *Instituto de Cosmetologia de Huixpan*

Border Patrol, 11, 77

Bowden, Charles, 10, 15, 116, 125

bracero program, 15

Buffalo Gap, Texas, 131–135

Buffalo Gap Church of Christ, 131–135, 142, 152

bus transportation, 19, 27–28; *colectivo*, 142–143; in Huixpan, 43; and maquiladora, 21, 69–70, 103, 109, 112, 113; to school, 88, 107

Calderón, Felipe, 11

cancer, 72, 93–94, 136, 156n3

child labor, 51–53, 59, 67

children, of Anay and Enrique: Elaine, 80, 82, 122, 128, 133, 140; Enrique (Kiké), 80, 82, 91, 99, 122, 135, 140; Eva, 26, 28, 75, 76, 81, 82, 83, 133–134, 140, 148; Juliet, 28, 75, 76, 81, 82, 133, 140

Church of Christ, 1, 25–26, 74, 75, 78. See also Buffalo Gap Church of Christ

Ciudad Juárez: history of, 8–11; location, 1, 7; maquiladora employees, numbers of, 12, 14–15, 68; name, 155n2; population of, 13, 18, 137–138; rainy season in, 27, 78; violence in, 7, 11, 13, 118–126, 135, 152–154

colonization, Spanish, 5, 6, 8, 21, 42, 84

Cortez, Hernán, 60, 157–158n3

cosmetology school. See Beauty School

cross-border solidarity. See solidarity march; Women in Black

cross-cultural communication, 5, 6, 78–79, 86

crosses, pink and black, 127, 128, 157n8

Davol Surgical Innovations, 92, 102, 105

Del Castillo, Adelaida, 22, 85

democratic Mexico, 8–9

dustry, 12–13, 89, 113, 137–138; education provided in, 69, 87–90; employee (line worker) stories, 109–113; employees' home/community, 18, 108–109; Enrique working in, 80, 113; feminicides, association with, 115–116; history of, 14–15; locations, 15; numbers of employees, 14, 15, 68; salary for line workers, 15, 17; "sweatshops," 16–17; women employment in, 21, 22, 23, 115
Margarita, 50, 51, 53
Margarito (Anay's uncle), 35–36
Medina, Alejandro, 111–112, 123
Merida Initiative, 12, 129
mestizo, 26, 157–158n3
missionary, 75–76, 78, 79–80, 140–142, 148. *See also* Buffalo Gap Church of Christ
Molloy, Molly, 116, 118, 125, 157n8

Nacho, *Profe*, 55, 56–58, 59
neolibral, 5, 6, 150, 156n4
nini, 120–121
Noemi (Anay's cousin), 33, 34, 56
North American Free Trade Agreement (NAFTA), 6–7, 22, 52, 156n5
nuegados, 45–46

Ofelia, 65–71: and Anay, 65–66; and Ciudad Juárez, 67; and Harnesses de Juárez, 68–80, 81

post-colonial feminist theory, 5–7, 149–150
Prepatoria Buenavista, 106, 107

ranchito, of Anay's grandparents, 29, 36–39
religions: Catholic, 34; Christian, 34, 59; Evangelical, 34, 60, 141–142; Protestant, 34, 141–142
Rio Grande/Rio Bravo, 1, 28, 77
Rogelio, *Profe*, 55, 56

Salinas de Gotari, Carlos, 6
Schutte, Ofelia, 4, 5, 6
Sicilia, Javier, 128–129
sobremesa, 41
solidarity march, 127
super-exploitation, 7, 17, 150
Suzi (Anay's brother's wife), 121, 152

unions, 21–22, 115
University of Texas at El Paso, 1, 92, 101, 123, 128

Valle Alta high school. *See* education, and Anay
visa, U.S. visitor, 132, 134, 151–152

Washington-Valdez, Diana, 116, 127
Women in Black, 127

yonke (auto junk yard), 25